I0448891

July 2013

INTERNET PHARMACIES

Federal Agencies and States Face Challenges Combating Rogue Sites, Particularly Those Abroad

GAO Highlights

Highlights of GAO-13-560, a report to congressional committees

INTERNET PHARMACIES

Federal Agencies and States Face Challenges Combating Rogue Sites, Particularly Those Abroad

Why GAO Did This Study

The Internet offers consumers a convenient method for purchasing drugs that is sometimes cheaper than buying from traditional brick-and-mortar pharmacies. According to a recent FDA survey, nearly 1 in 4 adult U.S. Internet consumers have purchased prescription drugs online. However, many Internet pharmacies are fraudulent enterprises that offer prescription drugs without a prescription and are not appropriately licensed. These rogue Internet pharmacies may sell drugs that are expired, improperly labeled, or are counterfeits of other drugs. A number of federal and state agencies share responsibility for administering and enforcing laws related to Internet pharmacies, including state boards of pharmacy, FDA, DOJ, CBP, and ICE.

The Food and Drug Administration Safety and Innovation Act directed GAO to report on problems with Internet pharmacies. This report identifies (1) how rogue sites violate federal and state laws, (2) challenges federal agencies face in investigating and prosecuting operators, (3) efforts to combat rogue Internet pharmacies, and (4) efforts to educate consumers about the risks of purchasing prescription drugs online. To conduct this work, GAO interviewed officials from FDA, DOJ, CBP, ICE, and other federal agencies, reviewed federal laws and regulations, and examined agency data and documents. GAO also interviewed officials from five state boards of pharmacy with varied approaches to regulating Internet pharmacies, and stakeholders including NABP, drug manufacturers, and companies that provide services to Internet businesses, such as payment processors.

View GAO-13-560. For more information, contact Marcia Crosse at (202) 512-7114 or CrosseM@gao.gov.

What GAO Found

Rogue Internet pharmacies violate a variety of federal and state laws. Most operate from abroad, and many illegally ship prescription drugs into the United States that have not been approved by the Food and Drug Administration (FDA), an agency within the Department of Health and Human Services (HHS), that is responsible for ensuring the safety and effectiveness of prescription drugs. Many also illegally sell prescription drugs without a prescription that meets federal and state requirements. Rogue sites also often violate other laws, including those related to fraud, money laundering, and intellectual property rights.

Rogue Internet pharmacies are often complex, global operations, and federal agencies face substantial challenges investigating and prosecuting those involved. According to federal agency officials, piecing together rogue Internet pharmacy operations can be difficult because they may be composed of thousands of related websites, and operators take steps to disguise their identities. Officials also face challenges investigating and prosecuting operators because they are often located abroad. The Department of Justice (DOJ) may not prosecute such cases due to competing priorities, the complexity of these operations, and challenges related to bringing charges under some federal laws.

Despite these challenges, federal and state agencies as well as stakeholders have taken actions to combat rogue Internet pharmacies. Federal agencies have conducted investigations that have led to convictions, fines, and asset seizures from rogue Internet pharmacies as well as from companies that provide services to them. FDA and other federal agencies have also collaborated with law enforcement agencies around the world to disrupt rogue Internet pharmacy operations. The Department of Homeland Security's (DHS) U.S. Customs and Border Protection (CBP) and U.S. Immigration and Customs Enforcement (ICE), which are responsible for enforcing laws related to the importation of goods such as prescription drugs, have also worked with other agencies, including FDA, to interdict rogue Internet pharmacy shipments at the border. Given that most rogue Internet pharmacies operate from abroad, states have faced challenges combating them, and generally focus their oversight on licensed in-state entities that fulfill orders for rogue Internet pharmacies. Companies that provide services to Internet-based businesses, such as search engines and payment processors, have also taken action—primarily by blocking services to them.

FDA and others have taken steps to educate consumers about the dangers of buying prescription drugs from rogue Internet pharmacies. FDA recently launched a national campaign to raise public awareness about the risks of purchasing drugs online, and the National Association of Boards of Pharmacy (NABP) posts information on its website about how to safely purchase drugs online. However, rogue Internet pharmacies use sophisticated marketing methods to appear legitimate, making it hard for consumers to differentiate between legitimate and rogue sites.

HHS, DOJ, and DHS provided technical comments on a draft of this report, which GAO incorporated as appropriate.

Contents

Abbreviations

CBP	U.S. Customs and Border Protection
CSA	Controlled Substances Act
CSIP	Center for Safe Internet Pharmacies
CTeL	Center for Telehealth and e-Health Law
DEA	Drug Enforcement Administration
DHS	Department of Homeland Security
DOJ	Department of Justice
FDA	Food and Drug Administration
FDCA	Federal Food, Drug, and Cosmetic Act
FSMB	Federation of State Medical Boards
FTC	Federal Trade Commission
IACC	International AntiCounterfeiting Coalition
ICE	U.S. Immigration and Customs Enforcement
IPEC	Intellectual Property Enforcement Coordinator
NABP	National Association of Boards of Pharmacy
USPIS	U.S. Postal Inspection Service
VIPPS	Verified Internet Pharmacy Practice Sites

GAO

U.S. GOVERNMENT ACCOUNTABILITY OFFICE

441 G St. N.W.
Washington, DC 20548

July 8, 2013

The Honorable Tom Harkin
Chairman
The Honorable Lamar Alexander
Ranking Member
Committee on Health, Education, Labor, and Pensions
United States Senate

The Honorable Fred Upton
Chairman
The Honorable Henry A. Waxman
Ranking Member
Committee on Energy and Commerce
U.S. House of Representatives

The Internet offers consumers a convenient method for purchasing prescription drugs that is sometimes cheaper than traditional brick-and-mortar retail pharmacies. Some Internet pharmacies are legitimate businesses that offer a safe and cost-effective way for consumers to obtain medications. However, there is mounting concern that many online pharmacies are, in fact, fraudulent enterprises. Commonly known as "rogue" websites, these fraudulent Internet pharmacies may send unsolicited e-mails offering cheap drugs without a prescription, advertise deep discounts that may seem too good to be true, and are often not licensed in the United States.[1] Buying drugs on the Internet is not uncommon. According to a recent survey conducted by the Food and Drug Administration (FDA), an agency within the Department of Health and Human Services, nearly one in four adult U.S. Internet consumers surveyed reported purchasing prescription drugs online.[2] At the same

---

[1] We refer to each website that fulfills first-time orders of prescription drugs as an Internet pharmacy, regardless of whether the company that operates the website is licensed as a pharmacy. We did not include in our review mail-order pharmacies or brick-and-mortar pharmacies that allow customers to request prescription drug refills online. Throughout this report, we use the term drugs to refer to prescription drugs; some Internet pharmacies may also sell over-the-counter drugs.

[2] FDA, "BeSafeRx Survey Highlights," http://www.fda.gov/Drugs/ResourcesForYou/Consumers/BuyingUsingMedicineSafely/BuyingMedicinesOvertheInternet/BeSafeRxKnowYourOnlinePharmacy/ucm318497.htm, accessed May 7, 2013.

time, nearly 30 percent said that they lacked confidence about how to safely purchase medicine online. This is a matter of grave concern as rogue Internet pharmacies may sell products that, among other things, have expired; been labeled, stored, or shipped improperly; and may even be counterfeits—unauthorized versions—of other drugs.

Like brick-and-mortar pharmacies, Internet pharmacies are subject to federal and state statutes and regulations that are designed to ensure the safety, efficacy, and proper administration of medications. A number of federal and state agencies share responsibility for regulating prescription drugs that are marketed and sold to U.S. consumers, including by Internet pharmacies. For example, FDA is responsible for ensuring the safety and effectiveness of prescription drugs, and FDA approval is required prior to marketing prescription drugs in the United States. The Department of Homeland Security's (DHS) U.S. Customs and Border Protection (CBP) is responsible for enforcing laws prohibiting the illegal importation of goods into the United States, including prescription drugs that have not been approved for marketing in the United States by FDA, and its U.S. Immigration and Customs Enforcement (ICE) conducts investigations related to violations of these laws, including illegally importing prescription drugs and trafficking in counterfeit goods. The U.S. Postal Inspection Service (USPIS) conducts investigations related to the misuse of mail. The Department of Justice (DOJ) may investigate and prosecute an operator of an Internet pharmacy that is suspected of violating federal laws. State agencies regulate the practice of pharmacy through state boards of pharmacy and, similarly, the practice of medicine though state medical boards.

The proliferation and widespread patronage of rogue Internet pharmacies has prompted public officials to identify them as a continuing public health threat. The Food and Drug Administration Safety and Innovation Act enacted in 2012 required that we report on problems posed by rogue Internet pharmacies.[3] This report identifies (1) how rogue Internet pharmacies are selling prescription drugs in violation of federal or state law or established industry standards, (2) challenges associated with federal investigations and prosecutions of rogue Internet pharmacies, (3) efforts to combat rogue Internet pharmacies, and (4) efforts to educate

---

[3]Pub. L. No. 112-144, § 1127, 126 Stat. 993, 1117-18 (2012).

consumers about the risks of rogue Internet pharmacies and how to recognize legitimate online pharmacies.

To identify how rogue Internet pharmacies are selling prescription drugs in violation of federal or state laws or established industry standards, we interviewed officials from federal agencies such as FDA, CBP, ICE, USPIS, and DOJ, reviewed federal laws and regulations, and examined agency documents, including those that presented information about federal indictments and prosecutions related to Internet pharmacy crimes. To obtain additional information, we interviewed a variety of knowledgeable stakeholders, including the National Association of Boards of Pharmacy (NABP) and LegitScript, an online pharmacy verification service, both of which routinely review Internet pharmacy websites to determine compliance with federal and state laws, and reviewed stakeholders' publications on rogue Internet pharmacies. (See app. I for a complete list of agencies and stakeholders interviewed.) In addition, we interviewed officials from state boards of pharmacy and state attorneys general offices and reviewed relevant pharmacy and medical practice laws and regulations of five judgmentally selected states—California, Florida, Maine, Nevada, and Utah. We selected these states on the basis of variations in the states' approaches in regulating Internet pharmacies.[4]

To identify challenges involved in investigating and prosecuting rogue Internet pharmacies, as well as efforts to combat rogue Internet pharmacies, we interviewed officials from federal agencies such as FDA, CBP, ICE, and DOJ. We obtained data from several federal agencies that summarize their efforts to combat Internet pharmacies. We discussed these data with agency officials, reviewed them for reasonableness and consistency, and determined that they were sufficiently reliable for our purposes. We also interviewed officials from the five state medical boards, four of those states' Attorneys General offices, as well as

---

[4]For example, California law prohibits the dispensing of drugs on the Internet without a prescription issued pursuant to a good-faith in-person medical examination, and authorizes the state to fine those that dispense violative prescriptions to California residents up to $25,000 per prescription. See Cal. Bus. & Prof. Code § 4067. The California Board of Pharmacy has taken action against those that have violated this law, for example, by dispensing drugs to California residents on the basis of a prescription issued pursuant to an online questionnaire. In contrast, Utah law allows licensed Internet pharmacies to dispense prescriptions for certain medications, such as specified erectile dysfunction drugs, hormone-based contraceptives, and smoking cessation drugs, on the basis of a prescription issued pursuant to an online questionnaire. See Utah Code Ann. ch. 58-83; Utah Admin. Code R156-83-306.

stakeholders with knowledge of state oversight activities, such as NABP, Federation of State Medical Boards (FSMB), the National Association of Attorneys General, and its Intellectual Property Committee. In addition, we interviewed officials from stakeholders involved in combating rogue Internet pharmacies, including the Alliance for Safe Online Pharmacies, Center for Safe Internet Pharmacies (CSIP), Pharmaceutical Security Institute, International AntiCounterfeiting Coalition (IACC), and the National Cyber-Forensics and Training Alliance. Stakeholders we also spoke with included officials from five drug manufacturers—Eli Lilly and Company; Merck & Co., Inc.; Pfizer; Purdue Pharma L.P.; and Takeda Pharmaceuticals U.S.A., Inc.—as well as several private companies that provide services to Internet-based companies, including the Internet registrar Go Daddy; search engines Microsoft and Google Inc. (Google); payment processors MasterCard International, Incorporated (MasterCard), Visa, Inc. (Visa), and PayPal; and the shipping companies FedEx and UPS. Finally, we reviewed published reports on rogue Internet pharmacy operations.

To identify efforts to educate consumers about the risks of rogue Internet pharmacies and how to recognize legitimate online pharmacies, we interviewed officials from federal agencies, as well as officials from stakeholders including NABP, FSMB, LegitScript, and the five manufacturers listed above to discuss their consumer education efforts. We also reviewed available educational campaign materials.

We conducted this performance audit from October 2012 to June 2013 in accordance with generally accepted government auditing standards. Those standards require that we plan and perform the audit to obtain sufficient, appropriate evidence to provide a reasonable basis for our findings and conclusions based on our audit objectives. We believe that the evidence obtained provides a reasonable basis for our findings and conclusions based on our audit objectives.

Background

The federal government plays a role in overseeing Internet pharmacy activity to the extent that these entities engage in interstate commerce or violate federal laws. However, states have traditionally regulated the practice of pharmacy and the practice of medicine. State boards of pharmacy license pharmacists and pharmacies, and state medical boards license physicians and set standards to ensure appropriate care, including standards for writing prescriptions. By violating federal and state laws, rogue Internet pharmacies threaten the public health.

Federal Role in Overseeing Internet Pharmacy Activity

No one federal agency is designated as the lead in combating rogue Internet pharmacy activity. Instead, several federal agencies, including FDA, CBP, and ICE, have separate and distinct roles and often work together.

Under the Federal Food, Drug, and Cosmetic Act (FDCA), FDA is responsible for ensuring the safety, effectiveness, and quality of domestic and imported prescription drugs that are marketed to U.S. consumers. The FDCA requires that certain drugs be dispensed pursuant to a prescription that is issued by a licensed practitioner.[5] The act also requires drug manufacturers to obtain FDA's approval before marketing their drugs in the United States.[6] To obtain FDA's approval, manufacturers must demonstrate to the agency that their drug is safe and effective for its intended use, and meet other statutory and regulatory standards relating to drug purity, labeling, manufacturing, and packaging.[7] Drugs that are manufactured in foreign countries for the U.S. market, including those sold over the Internet, are subject to the same requirements as those manufactured domestically. That is, all prescription drugs offered for import must meet the requirements of the FDCA, including requirements for obtaining FDA approval.[8] Drugs that are unapproved, or do not meet other provisions of the FDCA, such as those listed below, may be subject to enforcement action.

- Misbranded drugs include those that are sold without a prescription that meets applicable requirements, as well as those whose labeling or container is misleading or does not include required information, such as the name of the drug, adequate directions for use, and cautionary statements.[9]

---

[5]See 21 U.S.C. § 353(b). The FDCA, however, does not define how this requirement is to be met. Instead, each state's pharmacy and medical practice laws and regulations define what constitutes a valid prescription in that state.

[6]See 21 U.S.C. § 355(a).

[7]See, e.g., 21 U.S.C. § 355(d); 21 C.F.R. pts. 201, 210.

[8]See, e.g., 21 U.S.C. §§ 381, 384. In addition, drugs that are controlled substances also must meet the requirements of the Controlled Substances Import and Export Act. See 21 U.S.C. §§ 951-971.

[9]21 U.S.C. §§ 331(a), (b), 352, 353(b).

- Adulterated drugs include those that differ in strength, quality, or purity from approved products, as well as those that are not manufactured in conformity with good manufacturing practices.[10]

- Counterfeit drugs include those sold under a product name without proper authorization—where the drug is mislabeled in a way that suggests that it is the authentic and approved product—as well as unauthorized generic versions of FDA-approved drugs that mimic trademarked elements of such drugs.[11]

Drugs that do not appear to be in compliance with these provisions may be denied entry into the United States. In addition, those—including Internet pharmacy operators—that cause drugs to be misbranded, adulterated, or counterfeited, as well as those that sell such drugs, violate the FDCA and are subject to enforcement action.[12] Counterfeiting and trafficking or selling counterfeit drugs also violate laws that protect intellectual property rights.[13]

DOJ's Drug Enforcement Administration (DEA) is responsible for enforcing the Controlled Substances Act (CSA), which regulates the possession, manufacture, distribution, and dispensing of controlled substances, such as narcotic pain relievers.[14] DEA is also responsible for enforcing provisions and investigating violations of the Ryan Haight Online Pharmacy Consumer Protection Act of 2008, which amended the CSA to regulate the distribution and dispensing of controlled substances

---

[10]21 U.S.C. §§ 331(a), (b), 351.

[11]18 U.S.C. § 2320 prohibits trafficking in counterfeit drugs that mimic a trademarked drug through the use of a mark identical with or substantially indistinguishable from that of a trademarked drug, such as when a counterfeit drug uses the logo of a trademarked drug. See 18 U.S.C. § 2320(f)(6). 21 U.S.C. § 331(i)(3) prohibits any act that causes a drug to be a counterfeit drug, the sale or dispensing of a counterfeit drug, and the holding for sale or dispensing of a counterfeit drug. This provision applies regardless of whether the counterfeit product uses a logo, packaging, or other features identical to those of a trademarked drug. See 21 U.S.C. § 321(g)(2).

[12]See 21 U.S.C. §§ 331(a), (b), (c), (i), (k), 334(a).

[13]Intellectual property is any innovation, commercial or artistic, or any unique name, symbol, logo, or design used commercially. Intellectual property rights protect the economic interests of the creators of these works by giving them property rights over their creations. Generally, individual countries grant and enforce these rights.

[14]21 U.S.C. ch. 13.

on the Internet.[15] The act requires all entities that sell, or facilitate the sale, of controlled substances online to register and be authorized by the DEA to do so.[16] Entities based in foreign countries are not eligible for registration; it is illegal for consumers to import controlled substances. The act also defines what constitutes a valid prescription for controlled substances, and requires that such a prescription be issued for controlled substances dispensed over the Internet.[17]

CBP is responsible for enforcing laws prohibiting the illegal importation of goods into the United States, including prescription drugs that have not been approved by the FDA for the U.S. market, as well as those that are counterfeit or misbranded.[18] Additionally, the importation of prescription drugs by individuals for personal use is illegal, but FDA may exercise its regulatory discretion in determining whether to take enforcement action against such importation.[19] CBP coordinates with FDA to conduct inspections of products presented for import at the border. CBP interdicts and turns suspicious prescription drug shipments over to FDA for

---

[15]21 U.S.C. §§ 802(50)-(56), 829(e), 841(h) (amended by Pub. L. No. 110-425, 122 Stat. 4820 (2008)).

[16]21 U.S.C. §§ 823(f), 841(h).

[17]See 21 U.S.C. § 829(e). A valid prescription for a controlled substance is defined as one issued for a legitimate medical purpose in the usual course of professional practice by a practitioner who has conducted at least one in-person medical evaluation of the patient, or a covering practitioner (who conducts a medical evaluation at the request of a temporarily unavailable practitioner who had conducted an in-person medical evaluation of the patient within the past 24 months). Certain telemedicine practices are permitted in place of an in-person medical evaluation.

[18]19 U.S.C. § 1595a provides for seizure and forfeiture of merchandise offered for import contrary to law. 18 U.S.C. § 545 provides for criminal penalties for fraudulently or knowingly importing merchandise contrary to law as well as receiving, selling, or transporting merchandise known to have been imported contrary to law.

[19]FDA has established a policy that allows for the importation of noncontrolled prescription drugs for personal use under specified conditions, such as importing a small quantity (not more than a 90-day supply) of a drug that treats a serious condition and is not available domestically.

examination, and may seize and destroy certain shipments that are deemed to be in violation of applicable laws.[20]

ICE is responsible for, among other things, investigating violations of customs and trade laws, including those related to trafficking in counterfeit goods. ICE also operates the National Intellectual Property Rights Coordination Center, the mission of which is to share information across 17 federal government agencies and four foreign regulatory agencies, coordinate enforcement actions, and conduct investigations related to intellectual property theft—including those that occur through rogue Internet pharmacies.

USPIS helps prevent the illegal importation of prescription drugs by providing CBP with information about suspicious mail packages entering the United States. USPIS also investigates issues related to the misuse of mail.[21]

Other federal agencies are also sometimes involved in investigating rogue Internet pharmacy activity, to the extent that their jurisdiction relates to illicit activities conducted by these entities.

- The Internal Revenue Service investigates instances of money laundering, which is the act of disguising or concealing illicit funds to make them appear legitimate.[22]

---

[20]Shipments of prescription drugs that are seized by CBP are referred to ICE for investigation, and may also be referred to other federal law enforcement agencies for further investigation. In the absence of further investigation, CBP can take steps to destroy illegally imported controlled substances and counterfeit drugs. Under the FDCA, drugs that appear to be misbranded or adulterated are detained and importers have 90 days to overcome the appearance of an importation violation. If they choose not to do so or are unsuccessful, the importer can export the drugs out of the country, or they will be destroyed. See 21 U.S.C. § 381(a), (b). In 2012, the Food and Drug Administration Safety and Innovation Act provided FDA with authority to destroy without opportunity for export all imported drugs valued under $2,500 that are refused admission into the United States and do not overcome the appearance of an importation violation. See Pub. L. No. 112-144, § 708, 126 Stat. 993, 1068-69 (2012) (amending 21 U.S.C. § 381(a)). According to FDA officials, the agency is planning to implement this authority once it issues final regulations, which it is required to do by July 2014.

[21]For example, 18 U.S.C. § 1341 prohibits mail fraud.

[22]See 18 U.S.C § 1956.

GAO-13-560 Internet Pharmacies

- The Federal Trade Commission (FTC) may investigate rogue Internet pharmacies to the extent that their websites make false or misleading statements about how they collect and use medical information about consumers, which constitute violations of the Federal Trade Commission Act.[23] In addition, FTC may investigate potential violations of the CAN-SPAM Act of 2003, which imposes limitations and penalties on the transmission of certain unsolicited commercial e-mail, such as those with misleading information in the line identifying the person who sent the message.[24]

- DOJ's Federal Bureau of Investigation may investigate rogue Internet pharmacies if their activities defraud health care benefit programs or present a clear public health or safety threat.

DOJ prosecutes rogue Internet pharmacies through U.S. Attorneys' Offices located in 94 federal judicial districts throughout the nation, and through DOJ's Civil and Criminal Divisions, located in Washington, DC. U.S. Attorneys are the chief federal law enforcement officers for each federal district, and they serve as the nation's principal litigators under the direction of the Attorney General, working with officials from appropriate federal, state, local, and foreign agencies to prosecute rogue Internet pharmacy cases in their districts. DOJ's Civil and Criminal Divisions also prosecute such cases, coordinating closely with U.S. Attorneys, particularly in cases spanning multiple districts or international borders. DOJ's Civil Division has expertise in prosecuting cases involving FDCA violations, and DOJ's Criminal Division has expertise in prosecuting cases related to trafficking in counterfeit goods and offenses such as money laundering and fraud that are often integral to these criminal operations, as well as expertise in working with foreign law enforcement to obtain evidence or secure the extradition of defendants from other countries.

Other federal agencies have also undertaken efforts related to rogue Internet pharmacies, including by funding research related to how they operate, and by combating pharmaceutical counterfeiting.

---

[23]15 U.S.C. § 45 proh bits unfair or deceptive acts or practices that affect commerce. 15 U.S.C. § 52 prohibits the dissemination of false advertisements for the purpose of inducing the purchase of drugs and defines this conduct as an unfair or deceptive act or practice that affects commerce.

[24]15 U.S.C. §§ 7701-7713 (added by Pub. L. No. 108-187, 117 Stat. 2699 (2003)).

- The National Science Foundation has funded academic research that has demonstrated how rogue Internet pharmacies operate.

- The Intellectual Property Enforcement Coordinator (IPEC), within the Office of Management and Budget, has worked with federal agencies to develop strategies to combat pharmaceutical counterfeiting. It established an interagency working group on counterfeit pharmaceuticals, which, among other things, identified steps that the administration will take to combat the illicit sale of counterfeit drugs on the Internet. IPEC also issued a white paper to Congress which included legislative recommendations on how this goal could be achieved.[25] (For a summary of recent proposals related to combating rogue Internet pharmacies, see app. II.)

State Oversight of Pharmacies

In the United States, prescription drugs must be prescribed and dispensed by licensed health care professionals, who can help ensure proper dosing and administration and provide patients with important information on the drug's use. To legally dispense a prescription drug, a pharmacist licensed by the state and working in a pharmacy licensed by the state must be presented a valid prescription from a licensed health care professional. In addition, most states require pharmacies located outside their state to obtain a nonresident pharmacy permit prior to dispensing prescription drugs to customers located in that state. Some states regulate Internet pharmacies according to the same standards that apply to nonresident pharmacies. Others require pharmacies to obtain a special license in order to dispense prescription drugs ordered online.

The regulation of the practice of pharmacy is rooted in state pharmacy practice acts and regulations enforced by state boards of pharmacy. The state boards of pharmacy also are responsible for routinely inspecting pharmacies, ensuring that pharmacists and pharmacies comply with applicable state and federal laws, and investigating and disciplining those that fail to comply.

States also are responsible for regulating the practice of medicine. All states require that physicians practicing in the state be licensed to do so. State medical practice laws generally outline standards for the practice of

---

[25]See *Counterfeit Pharmaceutical Inter-Agency Working Group Report to the Vice President of the United States and to Congress* (Washington, D.C.: March 2011).

medicine and delegate the responsibility of regulating physicians to state medical boards. Each state's medical board also defines the elements of a valid patient—provider relationship, and grants prescribing privileges to physicians and other health care professionals. In addition, state medical boards investigate complaints and impose sanctions for violations of state medical practice laws.

Because regulation of the practices of pharmacy and medicine occurs at the state level, definitions and other requirements related to these practices differ from state to state. As a result, there is no uniform, national definition of the term "prescription" that applies to noncontrolled substances. Thus, certain activities, such as prescribing drugs without performing an in-person examination, may be explicitly illegal in one state while another state may not specifically address its legality.

Organizations such as NABP and FSMB have established and promoted uniform national standards related to Internet pharmacies for the consideration of state pharmacy and medical boards, as well as for consumers.

- NABP established the Verified Internet Pharmacy Practice Sites (VIPPS) program to provide a means for the public to identify legitimate Internet pharmacies. This accreditation program identifies those online pharmacies that are appropriately licensed, are legitimately operating via the Internet, and have successfully completed a review and inspection by NABP.[26]

- FSMB has developed model guidelines regarding the appropriate use of the Internet in medical practice. According to these guidelines, electronic technology should supplement and enhance, but not replace, the crucial interpersonal interactions that are the basis of the physician—patient relationship.[27] These professional standards, however, are not legally enforceable in the absence of state laws establishing such requirements.

---

[26]In reviewing websites for inclusion on its VIPPS list, NABP assesses compliance with the association's 11 Internet pharmacy standards, which include appropriate state licensure, lack of recent disciplinary action, and having operations that are based in the United States. NABP's VIPPS website can be accessed at http://vipps.nabp.net.

[27]Federation of State Medical Boards, *Model Guidelines for the Appropriate Use of the Internet in Medical Practice* (2002).

- The Center for Telehealth and e-Health Law (CTeL), an organization that works to overcome legal and regulatory barriers to telemedicine, issued guidance in February 2013 regarding how telemedicine, using two-way audio-video communications, can be used to establish a bona fide physician—patient relationship when prescribing noncontrolled substances.[28] Specifically, the guidance notes that an appropriate examination of the patient by the practitioner must occur prior to the issuance of a prescription, and that audio-only telephone conversations and e-mails cannot be used as a basis for establishing a bona fide practitioner—patient relationship.[29]

Public Health Risks Associated with Purchasing Prescription Drugs from Rogue Internet Pharmacies

Rogue Internet pharmacies often sell unapproved prescription drugs—including those that are substandard, counterfeit, and have no therapeutic value or are harmful to consumers.[30] These drugs may be manufactured under conditions that do not meet FDA standards, including unsanitary and unsterile conditions. The drugs sold by rogue Internet pharmacies have been found to contain too much, too little, or no active pharmaceutical ingredient, or the wrong active ingredient. They have also been found to contain dangerous contaminants, such as toxic yellow highway paint, heavy metals, and rat poison.[31]

Consumers who have taken prescription drugs purchased from rogue Internet pharmacies have experienced health problems, required

---

[28]Telemedicine is the use of electronic information and telecommunications technologies to support long-distance clinical health care, patient and professional health-related education, public health, and health administration through technologies such as videoconferencing.

[29]Center for Telehealth & e-Health Law, *Electronic Examination for Telemedicine Prescribing* (Washington, D.C.: Feb. 7, 2013).

[30]We previously reported on the safety risks that consumers face when purchasing drugs online. For example, we identified several problems associated with the handling, FDA approval status, and authenticity of drugs that we purchased from Internet pharmacies. See GAO, *Internet Pharmacies: Some Pose Safety Risks for Consumers*, GAO-04-820 (Washington, D.C.: June 17, 2004).

[31]See, for example, Partnership for Safe Medicines, "Hidden Poisons in Counterfeit Medicines," http://www.safemedicines.org/2012/03/no-drugs-at-all-.html, accessed June 12, 2013.

emergency treatments, and have died.[32] Because many rogue pharmacies sell prescription drugs without legitimate medical oversight, consumers may be harmed by ingesting drugs that are contraindicated for them, or have interactions with other medications that they are taking. However, adverse events caused by prescription drugs purchased from rogue Internet pharmacies are difficult to detect and quantify. Consumers may purchase drugs from rogue Internet pharmacies because of privacy concerns or to circumvent normal processes for obtaining prescription drugs. As a result, they may be reluctant to report health problems that they experience. Further, it can be difficult to determine whether adverse events are caused by substandard drugs. The role played by drugs from rogue Internet pharmacies may even go unnoticed. For example, when consumers take drugs that have no therapeutic value to treat their diseases, they may not experience adverse events to the drugs themselves, but they derive no benefit. Persistent symptoms may be attributed to their diseases, as opposed to ineffective treatments.

Rogue Internet Pharmacies Violate a Variety of Federal and State Laws

Rogue Internet pharmacies violate a variety of federal and state laws. Many ship unapproved drugs into the United States and sell drugs to consumers without a prescription that meets federal and state requirements. Rogue Internet pharmacies also violate other federal and state laws, such as those related to fraud and money laundering, in addition to not complying with industry standards.

---

[32]See, for example, FDA, "Buying Drugs Online: It's Convenient and Private, but Beware of 'Rogue Sites'," http://www.fda.gov/Drugs/EmergencyPreparedness/BioterrorismandDrugPreparedness/ucm137269.htm, accessed June 12, 2013; FDA, "FDA Alerts Consumers to Unsafe, Misrepresented Drugs Purchased Over the Internet," http://www.fda.gov/NewsEvents/Newsroom/PressAnnouncements/2007/ucm108846.htm, accessed June 12, 2013; and The Alliance for Safe Online Pharmacies, "Alliance for Safe Online Pharmacies' Response to the U.S. Intellectual Property Enforcement Coordinator's Request for Public Comment on the Development of the Joint Strategic Plan on Intellectual Property Enforcement" (Washington, D.C.: August 2012).

Most Rogue Internet Pharmacies Operate from Abroad, and Many Illegally Ship Unapproved Drugs into the United States and Sell Drugs without Requiring Valid Prescriptions

Although the exact number of rogue Internet pharmacies is unknown, most operate from abroad. According to LegitScript, an online pharmacy verification service that applies NABP standards to assess the legitimacy of Internet pharmacies, there were over 34,000 active rogue Internet pharmacies as of April 2013. Federal officials and other stakeholders we interviewed consistently told us that most rogue Internet pharmacies operate from abroad, and many have shipped drugs into the United States that are not approved by FDA. In doing so, they violate FDCA provisions that require FDA approval prior to marketing prescription drugs to U.S. consumers, as well as customs laws that prohibit the unlawful importation of goods, including unapproved drugs.[33] The prescription drugs that rogue Internet pharmacies sell have included counterfeit, misbranded, and adulterated drugs. Certain rogue Internet pharmacies have also sold dietary supplements that contain prescription drug ingredients, in violation of the FDCA. In addition, some, particularly those abroad, have sold controlled substances to customers located in the United States.[34] As no Internet pharmacies have been approved by DEA to dispense controlled substances to customers in the United States as of May 3, 2013, doing so violates the CSA.[35]

---

[33]See, e.g., 21 U.S.C. § 355(a); 18 U.S.C. § 545.

[34]For example, we purchased anabolic steroids, a controlled substance, from rogue Internet pharmacies as part of work conducted for a prior report. See GAO, *Anabolic Steroids Are Easily Purchased Without a Prescription and Present Significant Challenges to Law Enforcement Officials,* GAO-06-243R (Washington, D.C.: Nov. 3, 2005). More recently, in March 2013, nine individuals based in the United States were sentenced in the Northern District of California for their involvement in operating rogue Internet pharmacies that dispensed controlled substances to U.S.-based consumers from 2003 through 2007. See DOJ, "Nine Sentenced for Illegally Distributing Controlled Substances Over the Internet," http://www.justice.gov/usao/can/news/2013/2013_03_27_nine.sentenced.press.html, accessed June 14, 2013.

[35]See 21 U.S.C. § 952. In order to import controlled substances into the United States, a permit application must first be submitted to, and approved by DEA. See 21 C.F.R. §§ 1312.12-.13.

To sell drugs to their U.S. customers, foreign rogue Internet pharmacies use sophisticated methods to evade scrutiny by customs officials and smuggle their drugs into the country. For example, they have used intermediary shippers to help disguise the actual source of their shipments, which, according to CBP officials, may increase the likelihood that the shipments get through customs unnoticed. FDA and ICE officials told us that rogue Internet pharmacies have also misdeclared the contents of packages sent via express courier services or cargo shipments, in violation of customs laws.[36] Federal agencies use importation declarations to identify potentially illicit shipments for further examination; as such, misdeclaring the contents of such packages can result in illicit shipments evading additional scrutiny at the border. Further, rogue Internet pharmacies have disguised or hidden their drugs in various types of packaging; for example, CBP has found drugs in bottles of lotion and in tubes of toothpaste.[37]

---

[36]See, e.g., 18 U.S.C. §§ 542, 545.

[37]For a prior report, we purchased drugs from Internet pharmacies and received drugs that were also shipped in unconventional packaging, including in a plastic compact disc case and in a sealed aluminum can that was mislabeled. See GAO-04-820, 17.

Example of a Licensed Brick-and-Mortar Pharmacy Selling Misbranded Drugs

In 2011 and 2012, the owners of a U.S.-based brick-and-mortar pharmacy were convicted of several charges related to selling misbranded prescription drugs for rogue Internet pharmacies. The pharmacy was paid by multiple foreign rogue Internet pharmacies to fill prescriptions that did not meet state medical board requirements for a valid prescription and were sold and distributed in violation of the CSA. The rogue Internet pharmacies paid doctors, or in some cases, lay persons, to review brief online medical questionnaires and authorize the orders. The pharmacy filled orders for drugs, including controlled substances, and shipped them to customers who were usually located in a different state than the pharmacy. Because the drugs were sold without a valid prescription, they were considered misbranded, in violation of the FDCA.

Source: *United States v. Ihenacho et al.*, No. 08-CR-10337 (D. Mass. 2012).

Rogue Internet pharmacies also often sell drugs to consumers without a prescription, in violation of FDCA and state requirements, or with a prescription that does not satisfy FDCA and state requirements.[38] According to federal officials, they have done this by advertising that no prescription is necessary or by allowing consumers to purchase drugs after completing a brief online questionnaire that does not meet their state's requirements for a valid prescription. In some cases, rogue Internet pharmacies have ignored information from these questionnaires and have allowed consumers to make a purchase, regardless of the information disclosed. These actions violate the FDCA requirement that certain drugs be dispensed only with a prescription that is written by a licensed practitioner. In addition, some rogue Internet pharmacies operating from abroad have recruited doctors and pharmacies based and licensed in the United States to fulfill online prescription drug orders in exchange for payment, according to officials from federal agencies and stakeholders. Often, they have targeted doctors and pharmacies that are struggling financially, and have compensated them according to the number of prescriptions they authorize and fill, respectively. In these circumstances, the doctors violate state laws or medical board regulations as well as industry standards, such as those issued by FSMB and CTeL, which require valid patient—provider relationships prior to the issuance of a prescription. Likewise, the pharmacists violate state laws or pharmacy board regulations by selling drugs without ensuring that there is a prescription that meets state requirements. Drugs sold in this manner are considered misbranded, and are subject to enforcement under the FDCA.

Rogue Internet Pharmacies Violate a Variety of Other Federal and State Laws and Industry Standards

Rogue Internet pharmacies violate a variety of federal laws, including those related to fraud, money laundering, and intellectual property rights, according to officials from several federal agencies and stakeholders we interviewed. For example, rogue Internet pharmacies have engaged in mail fraud by using the mail to facilitate their illegal transactions.[39] In addition, some rogue Internet pharmacies have engaged in money laundering.[40] Specifically, to use the proceeds generated from rogue Internet pharmacies, operators have created a shell—or fake—company

---

[38]See 21 U.S.C. § 353(b).

[39]See 18 U.S.C. § 1341.

[40]See 18 U.S.C. § 1956.

to disguise the nature of their business, or have misstated the nature of their business to banks that process their credit card transactions, according to stakeholders we interviewed. To appear more legitimate to their consumers, rogue Internet pharmacies have also violated intellectual property laws by fraudulently displaying trademarks on their websites. For example, rogue Internet pharmacies have fraudulently displayed the VIPPS accreditation logo as well as the logos for payment processors such as Visa, MasterCard, or PayPal, without having obtained permission.[41] Rogue Internet pharmacies have violated a range of other federal laws, such as those related to making false or misleading statements, as well as by engaging in other deceptive and unfair acts or practices. For example, rogue Internet pharmacies have violated the CAN-SPAM Act by sending e-mails that list false information in the subject line or otherwise hide the message's origin.[42]

Rogue Internet pharmacies also violate state laws, including those related to operating without an appropriate license. Rogue Internet pharmacies have violated state laws by not obtaining pharmacy licenses from the states where their customers reside. In addition, licensed brick-and-mortar pharmacies recruited to fulfill prescription drug orders for rogue Internet pharmacies have violated state laws when they perform activities not authorized under their license or when they ship drugs to out-of-state customers. According to officials from state boards of pharmacy we interviewed, brick-and-mortar pharmacies have fulfilled online prescription drug orders, including to residents of another state without obtaining a nonresident pharmacy license in the state where those customers reside or without ensuring the prescriptions are valid.[43] When fulfilling such orders for out-of-state customers, brick-and-mortar pharmacies have also violated valid prescription requirements of the state where their customers live. For example, the California Board of Pharmacy identified an Internet pharmacy based in Utah that was violating California pharmacy laws,

---

[41]See 15 U.S.C. § 1114. According to one payment processor we interviewed, rogue Internet pharmacies that fraudulently display such trademarks may direct consumers to other websites, including those of their shell companies, to process such payments.

[42]See 15 U.S.C. § 7704.

[43]For example, Nevada requires out-of-state pharmacies that fill prescriptions placed over the Internet to be licensed in Nevada. See Nev. Rev. Stat. 639.2328, 639.23288. Officials from Nevada's Board of Pharmacy told us that a pharmacy would violate Nevada state law by shipping prescription drugs to Nevada residents without being licensed as a non-resident pharmacy.

which require that prescription drugs be dispensed through the Internet only with a prescription issued after a good-faith medical examination from a physician licensed in the state. According to the California Board of Pharmacy, the Utah pharmacy was selling prescription drugs to Californians based on prescriptions that it knew or should have known were not based on good-faith medical exams and were written by physicians who were not licensed in California, in violation of California law.[44] However, according to Utah Board of Pharmacy officials, the pharmacy was complying with Utah's laws, which allow certain licensed Internet pharmacies to dispense specified types of prescription drugs— such as certain erectile dysfunction drugs and hormone-based contraception—solely on the basis of an online questionnaire.[45]

Rogue Internet pharmacies do not comply with industry standards for legitimate Internet pharmacies. For example, officials from federal agencies and stakeholders told us that rogue Internet pharmacies have not provided accurate or complete information to domain name registrars when registering a website and have not adequately protected customer privacy.[46] In addition, rogue Internet pharmacies have not displayed identifying information on their website, such as a business address and telephone number.[47]

---

[44]See Cal. Bus. & Prof. Code § 4067(a).

[45]See Utah Code Ann. ch. 58-83; Utah Admin. Code R156-83-306.

[46]Domain name registrars are companies that sell domain name registration services to individuals and organizations so that they can use a specific website domain name, such as "www.gao.gov." We previously examined the extent to which individuals provide false information to domain name registrars when registering websites. See GAO, *Internet Management: Prevalence of False Contact Information for Registered Domain Names*, GAO-06-165 (Washington, D.C.: Nov. 4, 2005).

[47]In a prior report, we found that Internet pharmacies do not routinely disclose identifying information, and we suggested that Congress consider requiring Internet pharmacies to disclose such information. See GAO, *Internet Pharmacies: Adding Disclosure Requirements Would Aid State and Federal Oversight*, GAO-01-69 (Washington, D.C.: Oct. 19, 2000).

The Complex and Global Nature of Rogue Internet Pharmacies Poses Substantial Challenges for Federal Investigators and Prosecutors

Rogue Internet pharmacies are often complex, global operations, and as a result, federal agencies face substantial challenges investigating and prosecuting their operators.[48] Officials from federal agencies and stakeholders we interviewed told us that piecing together these operations can be difficult because rogue Internet pharmacies can be composed of thousands of related websites.[49] Although a small number of individuals own the majority of rogue Internet pharmacies operating across the world, they may contract with hundreds or thousands of individuals to set up, run, and advertise their websites—primarily by sending out unsolicited spam e-mails.[50] The ease with which operators can set up and take down websites also makes it difficult for agencies to identify, track, and monitor rogue websites and their activities, as websites can be created, modified, and deleted in a matter of minutes.

Additionally, rogue Internet pharmacies frequently locate different components of their operations in different countries, further complicating efforts to unravel the entirety of a rogue Internet pharmacy operation. For example, one rogue Internet pharmacy registered its domain name in Russia, used website servers[51] located in China and Brazil, processed payments through a bank in Azerbaijan, and shipped its prescription drugs from India.[52] (See fig. 1.)

---

[48]The challenges faced by federal investigators and prosecutors are not specific to rogue Internet pharmacies, but apply broadly to Internet crimes. In 2007, we reported that agencies face difficulties investigating and prosecuting cybercrimes and exercising jurisdiction over cybercriminals. GAO, *Cybercrime: Public and Private Entities Face Challenges in Addressing Cyber Threats*, GAO-07-705 (Washington, D.C.: June 22, 2007).

[49]For example, in 2012, FDA identified an Internet pharmacy operation that was composed of over 3,700 websites.

[50]Damon McCoy, et al., "PharmaLeaks: Understanding the Business of Online Pharmaceutical Affiliate Programs" (paper presented at the USENIX Security Symposium, Bellevue, WA, Aug. 8-10, 2012), accessed Oct. 1, 2012, http://www.cs.gmu.edu/~mccoy/papers/pharmaleaks.pdf. This study was funded in part by grants from the National Science Foundation.

[51]Website servers host and maintain the files of websites.

[52]Kirill Levchenko et al., "Click Trajectories: End-to-End Analysis of the Spam Value Chain" (paper presented at the Institute of Electrical and Electronics Engineers Symposium on Security and Privacy, Oakland, CA, May 22-25, 2011), accessed Oct. 1, 2012, http://cseweb.ucsd.edu/~savage/papers/Oakland11.pdf. This study was funded in part by grants from the National Science Foundation.

Figure 1: Map of a Rogue Internet Pharmacy Operation

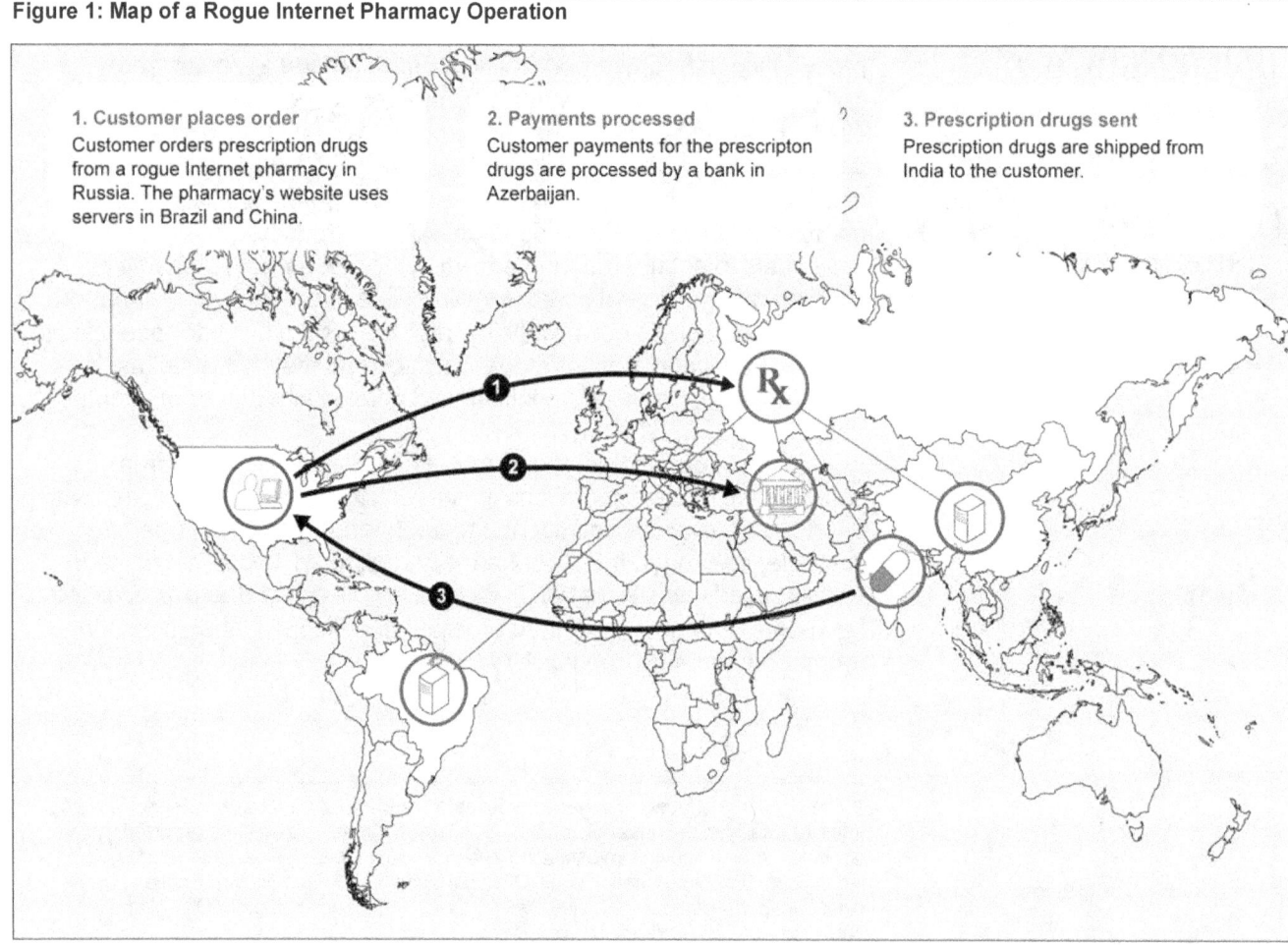

1. Customer places order
Customer orders prescription drugs from a rogue Internet pharmacy in Russia. The pharmacy's website uses servers in Brazil and China.

2. Payments processed
Customer payments for the prescripton drugs are processed by a bank in Azerbaijan.

3. Prescription drugs sent
Prescription drugs are shipped from India to the customer.

Source: Christian Kreibich, © 2011 Institute of Electrical and Electronics Engineers (data); Map Resources (map).

Notes: This figure is based on a figure that was published in Kirill Levchenko et al., "Click Trajectories: End-to-End Analysis of the Spam Value Chain" (paper presented at the Institute of Electrical and Electronics Engineers Symposium on Security and Privacy, Oakland, CA, May 22-25, 2011), accessed October 1, 2012, http://cseweb.ucsd.edu/~savage/papers/Oakland11.pdf. The study was funded in part by grants from the National Science Foundation.

Identifying rogue Internet pharmacy operators for investigation and possible prosecution can be challenging as they take steps to remain anonymous. According to officials from multiple federal agencies, rogue Internet pharmacy operators generally provide inaccurate contact information to domain name registrars and often use technological and other means to disguise their identities, physical locations, and affiliations with rogue Internet pharmacies. For example, rogue Internet pharmacies have often disguised their computer's Internet protocol address.[53]

Even when federal agencies are able to identify rogue Internet pharmacy operators, agency officials told us that they face jurisdictional challenges investigating and prosecuting them. Given the global nature of rogue Internet pharmacy operations, agencies may need assistance from foreign regulators or law enforcement in order to obtain information and gather evidence. However, rogue Internet pharmacies often deliberately and strategically locate components of their operations in countries that are unable or unwilling to aid U.S. agencies. In some instances, foreign regulators or law enforcement may be unwilling to take any action unless rogue Internet pharmacies are violating their country's laws. For example, certain countries' intellectual property rights laws are less stringent than those in the United States, and according to officials from federal agencies we interviewed, these countries' regulatory agencies have not always aided U.S. agencies with investigations into suspected prescription drug counterfeiters that have supplied rogue pharmacies. Additionally, some rogue Internet pharmacy operators may have political or other ties with foreign regulators or law enforcement, and requests by U.S. agencies for assistance would likely tip off operators and jeopardize investigations. In other cases, operators are located in countries that will not extradite them. Even when foreign law enforcement authorities are willing to aid investigations, they can be slow in responding to requests for help, according to officials from several federal agencies.

As a result of competing priorities and the complexity of rogue Internet pharmacies, federal prosecutors may not always prosecute these cases. In determining whether to pursue cases, U.S. Attorneys consider a number of factors, including the federal government's jurisdiction over the crime, the type and seriousness of the offense, the number and location of victims, the sufficiency of the evidence, as well as the district's prosecutorial priorities and resources. According to officials from multiple federal agencies, prosecutors may not be inclined to pursue rogue Internet pharmacy cases. Operators are often located outside the jurisdiction of U.S. courts, the number and location of victims is frequently unknown, and pursuing these cases is resource intensive as they often

---

[53]An Internet protocol address is a sequence of numbers that provides a description of the location of networked computers and distinguishes one computer from another on the Internet, similar to a physical street address.

involve the application of specialized investigative techniques, such as undercover work and Internet forensics. Further, U.S. Attorneys' Offices will also often prioritize cases for prosecution by applying minimum thresholds associated with illicit activities, in order to focus their limited resources on the most serious crimes. For example, when determining whether to pursue rogue Internet pharmacy cases, certain U.S. Attorneys' Offices may impose thresholds related to the quantity or monetary value of illicitly sold prescription drugs. According to officials at a number of agencies, the agencies may not pursue investigations of cases that they believe do not meet the minimum thresholds established by the U.S. Attorneys for their districts, and similarly, the U.S. Attorneys' Offices may not pursue cases for the same reason.

Basing a prosecution on violations of the FDCA can also be challenging, which may contribute to prosecutors declining to pursue rogue Internet pharmacy cases. Though rogue Internet pharmacy activity clearly violates the FDCA, proving violations of the act's misbranding and counterfeiting provisions can be difficult, according to a DOJ official.[54] In addition, violations of these provisions of the FDCA are subject to relatively light criminal penalties, which may limit prosecutors' interest. When federal prosecutors pursue charges against rogue Internet pharmacy operators, they often charge them for violating other laws, such as smuggling, mail fraud, wire fraud, or money laundering, since such violations can be less onerous to prove and carry stronger penalties.[55]

---

[54]For example, to federally prosecute rogue Internet pharmacies for misbranding violations as a result of dispensing drugs without a prescription that meets FDCA requirements, prosecutors need to prove that the pharmacies violated specific state laws that outline requirements for valid prescriptions. According to a DOJ official, identifying the state laws that best match the circumstances of each case can be a time-consuming process.

[55]See, e.g., 18 U.S.C. §§ 545 (smuggling), 1341 (mail fraud), 1343 (wire fraud), 1956 (money laundering). These crimes are subject to penalties of up to 20-30 years in jail or fines ranging from $500,000 to $1 million, or both. Violations of FDCA misbranding and counterfeiting provisions are subject to maximum penalties of 3 years in jail or a fine of $10,000, or both, under 21 U.S.C. § 333, and 18 U.S.C. § 3571 provides for a $250,000 fine or twice the gross gain or loss for individual defendants for all felony violations, including FDCA felony violations.

Federal Agencies, States, and Stakeholders Have Taken a Variety of Steps to Combat Rogue Internet Pharmacies

Federal agencies, states, and stakeholders have investigated and prosecuted operators, prevented illicit shipments of pharmaceuticals from entering the United States, and blocked rogue Internet pharmacies' ability to market and sell their products.

Federal Agencies Have Investigated and Prosecuted Rogue Internet Pharmacy Operators and Prevented Some Illegal Shipments

Despite facing substantial challenges, several federal agencies—including FDA, ICE, and USPIS—have investigated and prosecuted rogue Internet pharmacy operators that have violated federal laws. (See fig. 2 for a screenshot of a rogue Internet pharmacy that FDA recently investigated, which led to a conviction in 2011.) Agencies have investigated rogue Internet pharmacies independently and conducted collaborative investigations with other federal agencies through ICE's National Intellectual Property Rights Coordination Center. In certain instances, agencies have collaborated with international law enforcement agencies. Agency investigations have resulted in the conviction of operators, fines, and asset seizures. Specifically, according to agency officials, from fiscal years 2010 through 2012,

- FDA opened 227 rogue Internet pharmacy investigations and its investigations led to the conviction of 219 individuals and more than $76 million in fines and restitution;[56]

- ICE initiated 138 investigations and its investigations led to 56 convictions and the seizure of nearly $7 million;[57]

- USPIS worked on 392 investigations and arrested 560 individuals;

---

[56]Data on FDA investigations represent the agency's Internet-related investigations into the illicit distribution of prescription drugs, drug ingredients, medical devices, and dietary supplements that are tainted with prescription drug ingredients and include investigations into companies that aid and abet rogue pharmacy operations.

[57]Data on ICE investigations represent all agency investigations into the illicit importation of prescription drugs. ICE officials estimate that more than half of these investigations involve rogue Internet pharmacies.

- IRS conducted 22 investigations and its investigations led to the conviction of 5 individuals; and

- DEA conducted 49 investigations into rogue Internet pharmacies and seized more than $1 million.[58]

---

[58]The data provided by individual agencies includes investigations that were conducted in collaboration with other federal agencies, and, accordingly, cannot be totaled. Since rogue online pharmacies may be prosecuted under a variety of federal statutes, including mail fraud, trafficking in counterfeit goods, and customs violations, or violations of the FDCA or CSA, we were unable to obtain data on the number of prosecutions of rogue Internet pharmacy operators.

Figure 2: Screenshot of a Rogue Internet Pharmacy Website That Sold Counterfeit and Misbranded Drugs, 2006

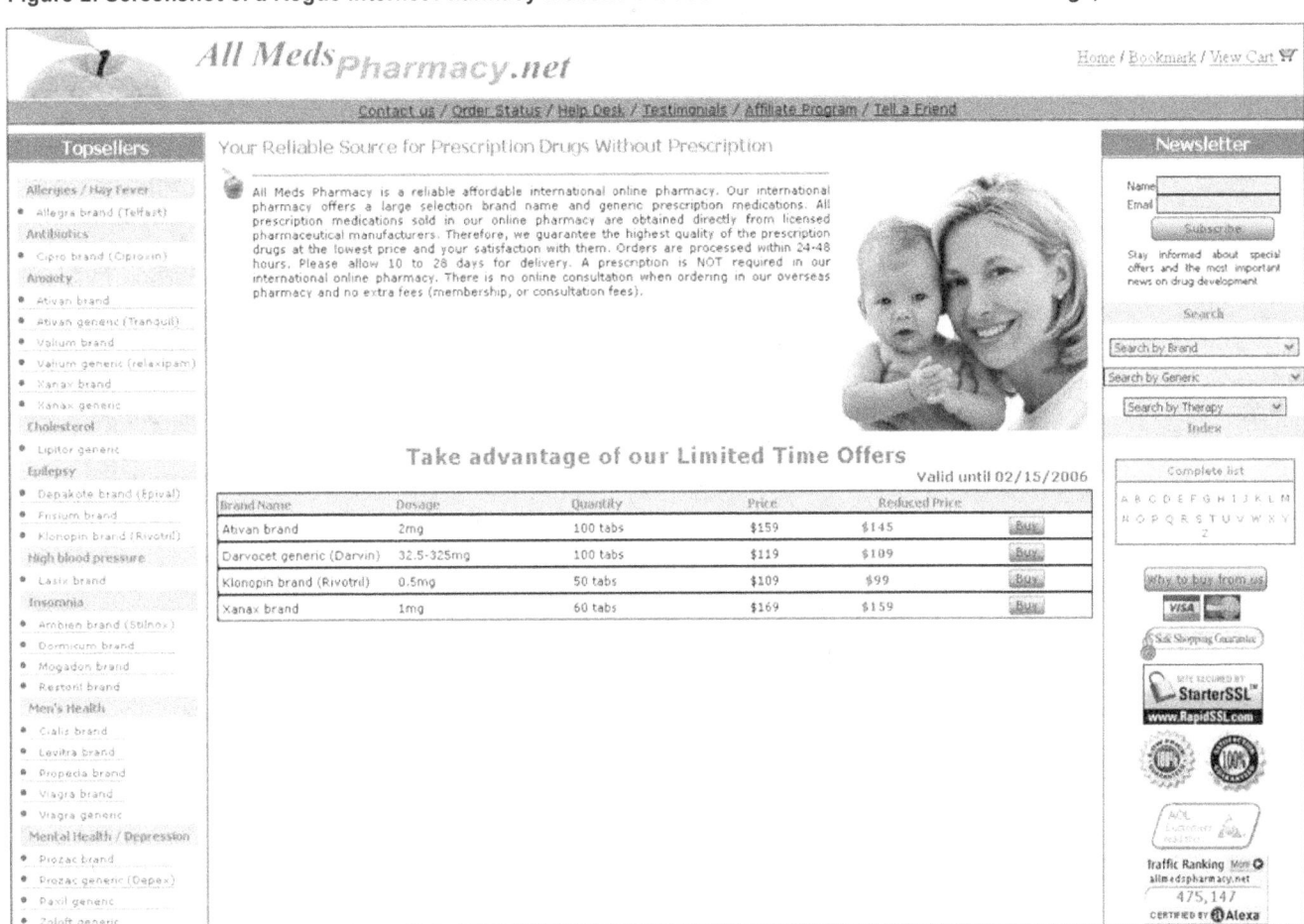

Source: Internet Archive.

Notes: The Food and Drug Administration conducted an investigation into www.allmedspharmacy.net, and discovered that this website sold counterfeit and misbranded drugs, including controlled substances. We reviewed agency press releases, the indictment, and the court's judgment related to this investigation. One of the website's operators was located in Costa Rica and drugs were shipped into the United States from Pakistan. The operator also maintained a customer service call center in the Philippines and received payments from customers via payment processors located in the Netherlands. In conducting this investigation, FDA collaborated with Costa Rica law enforcement officials as well as Interpol. The operator was extradited to the United States and pled guilty to charges of conspiracy to defraud the United States through the sale of misbranded and counterfeit drugs and conspiracy to traffic in controlled substances. The operator was sentenced in June 2011 to 4 years in federal prison and ordered to forfeit $850,829.60. The second operator is a citizen of Canada and remained a fugitive as of January 2011. *United States v. Calvelo et al.*, No. 08-CR-20167 (D. Kan. 2011).

The image displayed is a screenshot of the www.allmedspharmacy.net website as of February 3, 2006, as retrieved from http://web.archive.org/web/20060203035725/http://www.allmedspharmacy.net/home/default.aspx on June 5, 2013.

In addition to investigating rogue Internet pharmacy operators, federal agencies have investigated companies for providing services to rogue Internet pharmacies. In 2011, a DOJ and FDA investigation led to a settlement under which Google agreed to forfeit $500 million for allowing certain rogue Internet pharmacies to place sponsored advertisements in its search engine results from calendar years 2003 through 2009.[59] In March 2013, a DOJ investigation led to a settlement under which UPS agreed to forfeit $40 million for transporting and distributing prescription drugs, including controlled substances, from certain rogue Internet pharmacies to U.S. consumers from calendar years 2003 through 2010.[60] As part of their settlements with DOJ, both companies noted that they will stop serving rogue Internet pharmacies and create compliance programs to identify rogue actors, in exchange for not being prosecuted by the U.S. government for crimes related to this activity. In addition, according to FedEx documents, DOJ is investigating the company for potentially violating federal law by shipping prescription drugs from Internet pharmacies.

Federal agencies have also taken steps to shut down rogue Internet pharmacy websites. For example, FDA and other federal agencies have participated in Operation Pangea, an annual worldwide, week-long initiative in which regulatory and law enforcement agencies from around the world work together to combat rogue Internet pharmacies. In 2013, FDA took action against 1,677 rogue Internet pharmacy websites during Operation Pangea. In 2012, as part of the Operation, FDA informed domain name registrars that over 4,100 rogue Internet pharmacy websites were illegally selling prescription drugs online, in violation of the registrars' terms of service with their customers.[61] The agency informed the registrars of these violations in order to encourage them to shut down these violative websites. FDA officials told us that the effect of such

---

[59]Google forfeited the gross revenue it received as payment for such advertisements, along with the gross revenue made by the rogue Internet pharmacies from their sales to U.S. customers.

[60]UPS forfeited the gross revenue it received as payments from rogue Internet pharmacies for shipping their parcels.

[61]According to FDA and DEA officials, they do not have the authority under the FDCA or CSA to seize rogue Internet pharmacy websites and shut them down. FDA officials told us that they inform domain name registrars of websites engaged in illicit activity so that the registrars can voluntarily take action to cease providing services to them, or they may work with DOJ to take action.

shutdowns is primarily disruptive since rogue Internet pharmacies often reopen after their websites get shut down; officials from federal agencies and stakeholders we spoke with likened shutting down websites to taking a "whack-a-mole" approach. One stakeholder noted that rogue Internet pharmacies own and keep domain names in reserve so that they can redirect traffic to new websites and maintain operations if any of their websites get shut down. Rogue Internet pharmacies may also find new registrars to host their websites—figure 3 provides an example of a rogue Internet pharmacy website that was shut down during Pangea but that continued operations by switching to another domain name registrar. FDA has also issued warning letters to rogue Internet pharmacies to notify them that they are engaged in potentially illegal activity and direct them to cease their illegal activity.[62] From calendar years 2009 through 2012, FDA reported issuing about 30 warning letters to rogue Internet pharmacies. According to FDA officials, rogue Internet pharmacies often ignore the letters and continue with their illicit activity. However, in some cases, FDA's warning letters have led to the removal of potentially dangerous products from certain websites.[63] FDA officials told us that they remain committed to combating rogue Internet pharmacies and in April 2013 they formed a new Cyber Crimes Investigation Unit that is devoted to this cause.

---

[62]When FDA determines that an entity has significantly violated the FDCA, the agency notifies the entity through a warning letter. The letter directs the entity to correct the problem within a specified time frame.

[63]For example, FDA issued warning letters in May 2012 to two Internet pharmacies that were offering alitretinoin for sale to U.S. consumers because FDA felt the websites presented a significant public health risk. Alitretinoin is an unapproved drug that is potentially dangerous because it has the potential to cause severe birth defects if taken by pregnant women. In response to the warning letters, the websites stopped offering the drug for sale.

Figure 3: Screenshot of a Rogue Internet Pharmacy Website That Received a Warning Letter from FDA in 2012 as Part of Operation Pangea

Source: Internet Archive.

Notes: In September 2012, the Food and Drug Administration (FDA) sent a warning letter to the operator of www.canadadrugs.com, notifying it that the agency had determined that this website and 3,712 others that the operator ran were supplying unapproved and misbranded prescription drugs for sale to consumers in the United States. We reviewed FDA's warning letter and spoke with agency

　　　　　　　　　　　　　GAO-13-560 Internet Pharmacies

officials about its investigation. (FDA's warning letter can be found at http://www.fda.gov/ICECI/EnforcementActions/WarningLetters/2012/ucm321068.htm, accessed Apr.18, 2013.) As part of Operation Pangea, FDA informed the domain name registrar that these websites were illegally selling prescription drugs, and according to agency officials, the registrar shut down these sites in response. However, according to FDA officials, shortly after Pangea, the websites' operator registered its domain names with a new registrar, and as a result, the sites are operational as of April 2013.

The image displayed is a screenshot of the www.canadadrugs.com website as of September 19, 2012, as retrieved from http://web.archive.org/web/20120919225427/http://www.canadadrugs.com/ on June 5, 2013.

Federal agencies responsible for preventing illegal prescription drug imports have also interdicted rogue Internet pharmacy shipments. CBP coordinates with FDA to inspect and seize illicit mail, express courier, and cargo shipments of prescription drugs presented for import at the border on a daily basis. CBP also leads Operation Safeguard, a multiagency initiative to target illicit imports of prescription drugs. Once a month, CBP, along with FDA and ICE, targets a specific international mail or express courier facility and, according to agency officials, conducts extensive examinations and seizures of illicit prescription drug shipments for 3 days. In total, from fiscal years 2010 through 2012, FDA reported examining nearly 45,000 shipments and CBP reported seizing more than 14,000 illicit shipments of prescription drugs, with mail shipments constituting the majority of the shipments that were seized. In addition to seizures of shipments presented for import, according to USPIS, the agency seized more than 800 illicit shipments of controlled substances in the domestic mail system during fiscal year 2012. Despite these efforts, FDA officials told us that the sheer volume of inbound international mail shipments—which total nearly 1.2 million pieces every day, according to USPIS—makes it difficult to interdict all illicit prescription drug imports.[64]

Other federal agencies have also taken steps to combat rogue Internet pharmacies by sponsoring research and engaging stakeholders. The National Science Foundation has provided grants to researchers who have examined rogue Internet pharmacy operations and developed strategies for combating them. For example, researchers found that rogue Internet pharmacies may be vulnerable to efforts to limit their ability to

[64]Data represent the average daily number of inbound parcels from November 1, 2011, to October 31, 2012. We also previously reported that the large number of illicit prescription drug shipments imported through the mail prevents agencies from being able to interdict all incoming shipments of illicit drugs. See GAO, *Prescription Drugs: Strategic Framework Would Promote Accountability and Enhance Efforts to Enforce the Prohibitions on Personal Importation*, GAO-05-372 (Washington, D.C.: Sept. 8, 2005).

process online payments.[65] In addition, IPEC has worked with private companies to encourage them to limit services to rogue Internet pharmacies.

While DEA has investigated and taken actions to combat rogue Internet pharmacies that have violated the CSA, the agency has recently decreased the priority it places on combating them. According to agency officials, the criminal penalties associated with the Ryan Haight Act, which was implemented in 2009, have substantially reduced the extent to which controlled substances are sold online, as domestic pharmacies have stopped fulfilling orders on behalf of rogue Internet pharmacies.[66] In addition, agency officials told us that while rogue Internet pharmacies may still advertise the sale of controlled substances, they often do not actually sell them. DEA officials based this conclusion on the agency's 2011 assessment of 10 rogue Internet pharmacies that advertised the sale of controlled substances, through which it found that 4 of the 10 sold such substances.[67] Further, according to DEA officials, foreign rogue Internet pharmacies that sell controlled substances do not actually sell the most dangerous and addictive substances, and DEA has limited extraterritorial jurisdiction over the distribution of these types of drugs.[68] DEA officials also told us that results from their fieldwork support the

[65]Damon McCoy, et al., "Priceless: The Role of Payments in Abuse-advertised Goods" (paper presented at the ACM Conference on Computer and Communications Security, Raleigh, NC, Oct. 16-18, 2012), http://www.cs.gmu.edu/~mccoy/papers/CCS12Priceless.pdf, accessed Oct. 24, 2012. This study was funded in part by grants from the National Science Foundation.

[66]According to DEA officials, illicit pain clinics—brick-and-mortar operations where customers can obtain prescriptions for controlled substances without a legitimate medical need—have since emerged as the primary source of controlled substance diversion.

[67]DEA officials randomly selected websites to examine from a 2011 LegitScript report that included a sample list of 1,000 rogue Internet pharmacies that had advertised the sale of controlled substances. See LegitScript, *Drug Dealers on the Internet: Is the DEA enforcing the Ryan Haight Act?* (Portland, OR: June 2011).

[68]A controlled substance is classified on the basis of whether the drug has a currently accepted medical use in treatment in the United States and its relative abuse potential and likelihood of causing dependence. The classification system includes five schedules and their order reflects substances that are progressively less dangerous and addictive. See 21 U.S.C. § 812. DEA has extraterritorial jurisdiction over individuals that manufacture or distribute schedule I and II controlled substances—those that are the most dangerous and addictive—outside the territorial jurisdiction of the United States who intend to unlawfully import the substances or know that they will be unlawfully imported, but this extraterritorial jurisdiction does not apply to controlled substances on other schedules. See 21 U.S.C. § 959.

agency's conclusion that domestic and foreign rogue Internet pharmacies are generally not selling controlled substances. Furthermore, agency officials told us that they do not track data that could demonstrate a reduction in the sale of controlled substances online because they told us there is no reason to do so. DEA officials explained their rationale by saying that the agency does not collect data on threats that do not exist. However, DEA's 2011 assessment of Internet pharmacies that advertised the sale of controlled substances revealed that 40 percent were selling such substances. DEA has not gathered additional data to demonstrate the extent to which controlled substances are being diverted over the Internet.[69]

States Face Challenges Combating Rogue Internet Pharmacies, and Have Focused on Regulating the Activities of Licensed Pharmacies

States face challenges investigating rogue Internet pharmacies and have played a limited role in combating them. Given that most rogue Internet pharmacies operate from abroad, stakeholders including NABP, National Alliance for Model State Drug Laws, and National Association of Attorneys General, as well as officials from several state attorneys general offices told us that states do not have the authority, ability, or resources to investigate and prosecute them. These stakeholders told us that, as a result, states generally have not investigated rogue Internet pharmacies for violating their laws. In addition, officials from the five state boards of pharmacy we interviewed also told us that they do not proactively investigate unlicensed pharmacy activity, and most of the boards view the enforcement of unlicensed pharmacy activity as the responsibility of state law enforcement agencies, rather than themselves. Accordingly, they have not actively sought to identify or investigate rogue Internet pharmacies—either in-state or out-of-state—that sell prescription drugs to customers within their state, though they may look into rogue Internet pharmacies if they received complaints. Further, board officials told us that they face challenges enforcing laws outside of their own states. When rogue Internet pharmacies located in other states violate their state laws, board officials contact officials of state boards where the pharmacies are located, and it is then the responsibility of the contacted boards to take any appropriate investigative or enforcement actions. The boards may also send cease-and-desist letters or attempt to fine out-of-

---

[69]In 2011, we recommended that DEA take steps to better capture data on the agency's efforts to reduce the diversion of controlled substances. See GAO, *Prescription Drug Control: DEA Has Enhanced Efforts to Combat Diversion, but Could Better Assess and Report Program Results*, GAO-11-744 (Washington, D.C.: Aug. 26, 2011).

state pharmacies that violate their states' laws. However, the boards have no ability to ensure compliance with enforcement actions against pharmacies outside of their state that are not licensed in their state.

State boards of pharmacy focus on regulating licensed brick-and-mortar pharmacies located within their state. In regulating licensed pharmacies, officials from each of the five states told us that they have taken enforcement actions against licensed pharmacies in their states for fulfilling orders on behalf of rogue Internet pharmacies or illicitly selling prescription drugs over the Internet. For example, in 2010, the Nevada Board of Pharmacy revoked the license of a pharmacist for illegally shipping controlled substances to an out-of-state customer who placed an order through a rogue Internet pharmacy. In addition to actions taken by state pharmacy boards, state medical boards have also taken enforcement actions against physicians involved in illicitly writing prescriptions for rogue Internet pharmacies, according to FSMB officials.[70]

Stakeholders Have Blocked Services to Known Rogue Internet Pharmacies and Routinely Share Information with Federal Agencies

Stakeholders that provide services to Internet-based businesses have blocked rogue Internet pharmacies' ability to market and sell their products. These stakeholders have taken such actions on the basis of information that they learn about and share through various associations.

- CSIP has helped member companies that provide services to Internet businesses—such as Internet registrars, search engines, and payment processors—share information about rogue Internet pharmacies, and encourages its members to block services to them.[71] CSIP contracts with a third-party company that proactively searches the Internet to identify rogue Internet pharmacies and disseminates this information to its members. In addition, CSIP gathers information about rogue Internet pharmacies from member companies, as well as from other outside sources such as federal agencies. According to CSIP, from November 1, 2011, through December 1, 2012, its members took more than 3 million actions against rogue Internet

[70]In addition to the limited role played by states, state officials and stakeholders that we spoke with were generally unaware of any efforts by local governments to combat rogue Internet pharmacies.

[71]IPEC worked with CSIP's member companies to encourage and help facilitate the creation of the association.

pharmacies. For example, Internet registrars shut down rogue Internet pharmacy websites, search engines prevented them from placing advertisements, and credit card companies prevented payments from being processed.[72]

- IACC has also taken action to combat rogue Internet pharmacies by, among other things, working with credit card companies to discourage banks from processing payments for rogue Internet pharmacies.[73] IACC officials told us that they collect information on websites that market counterfeit and otherwise illegal products from trademark and copyright holders, including four brand-name prescription drug manufacturers. IACC then provides this information to credit card companies so that they can take action against banks that process payments for these rogue Internet pharmacies. (See fig. 4.) Under their terms of service, credit card companies can fine or take other enforcement actions against banks that process payments for merchants involved in illegal activities.

---

[72]The 3 million actions taken by CSIP members may include actions taken by multiple members against a single rogue Internet pharmacy.

[73]Certain credit card companies contract with banks to issue credit cards and to authorize merchants to accept those cards.

Figure 4: Payment Processing Interventions Used to Combat Rogue Internet Pharmacies

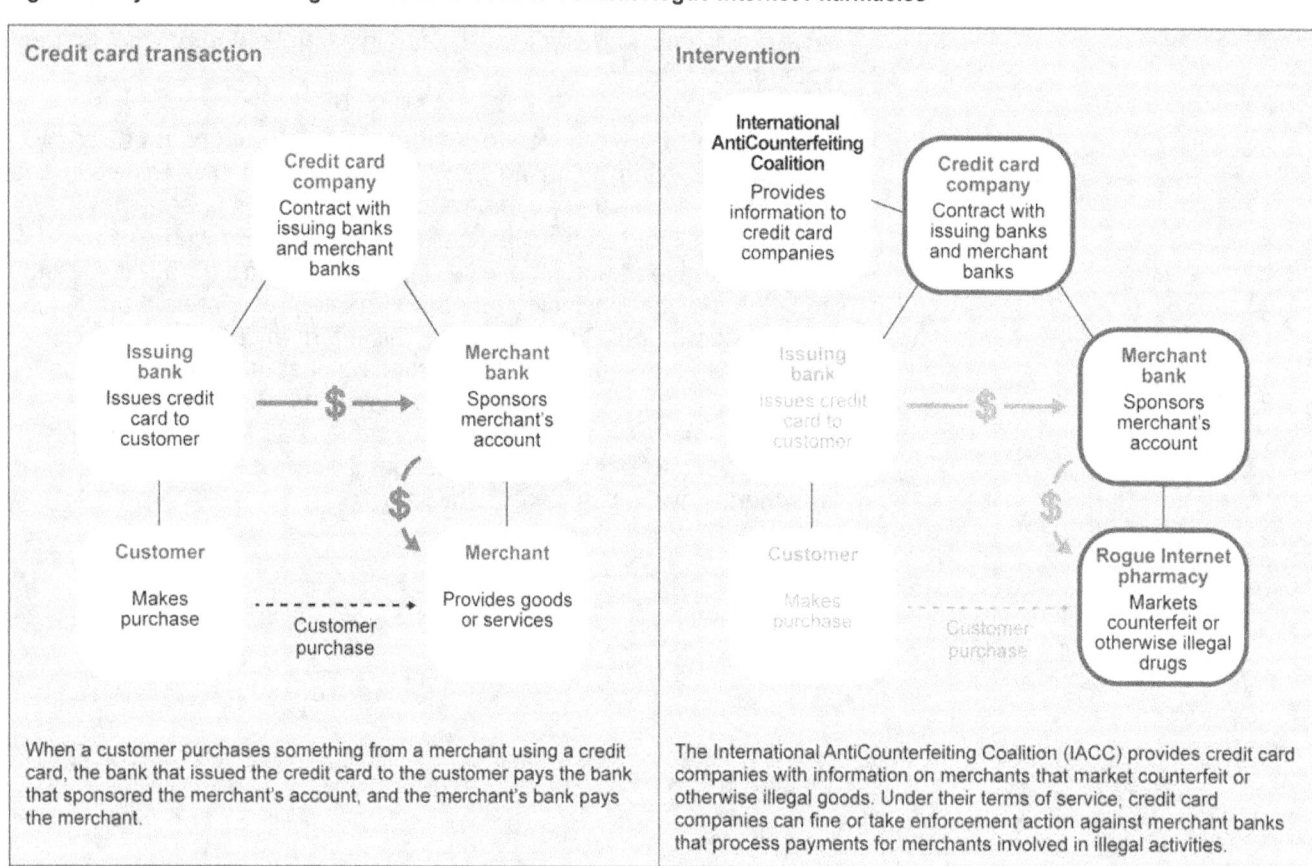

Credit card transaction

When a customer purchases something from a merchant using a credit card, the bank that issued the credit card to the customer pays the bank that sponsored the merchant's account, and the merchant's bank pays the merchant.

Intervention

The International AntiCounterfeiting Coalition (IACC) provides credit card companies with information on merchants that market counterfeit or otherwise illegal goods. Under their terms of service, credit card companies can fine or take enforcement action against merchant banks that process payments for merchants involved in illegal activities.

Source: GAO.

In addition to private efforts to block services to rogue Internet pharmacies, drug manufacturers maintain surveillance programs to identify and investigate the marketing of counterfeit versions of their brand-name prescription drugs and share their findings with federal agencies. In doing so, they monitor web activity to identify rogue Internet pharmacies, and employ investigators to gather evidence against rogue operators. On the basis of their investigations, these manufacturers provide federal agencies, such as ICE and FDA, with investigative leads and information that may support existing investigations. In addition, manufacturers have also provided CBP with information to better target illicit drug imports and with brochures to help CBP officials differentiate between legitimate and counterfeit prescription drugs.[74]

Several stakeholders also help facilitate information sharing between drug manufacturers and federal agencies on rogue Internet pharmacies. The Pharmaceutical Security Institute, an association of 26 drug manufacturers focused on sharing information related to counterfeit prescription drugs, collects and analyzes surveillance information from its members and, according to an official from the institute, helps them share information with federal agencies about the illicit marketing of counterfeit prescription drugs by rogue Internet pharmacies. The National Cyber-Forensics & Training Alliance—an organization that facilitates public-private information sharing on cybercrime—also works with drug manufacturers to share information with federal agencies. Officials said that the alliance collects information from the manufacturers and performs additional intelligence gathering to provide agencies with actionable investigative leads, such as the identities and locations of operators.

FDA and Stakeholders Have Taken Steps to Educate Consumers about the Risks of Purchasing Prescription Drugs from Internet Pharmacies, but Challenges Remain

FDA and stakeholders have taken steps to educate consumers about the dangers of buying prescription drugs from rogue Internet pharmacies and how to identify legitimate ones; however, these efforts face challenges. In September 2012, FDA launched a national campaign called "BeSafeRx: Know Your Online Pharmacy" to raise public awareness and educate consumers about the risks associated with purchasing prescription drugs on the Internet. The campaign provides information about the dangers of purchasing drugs from rogue Internet pharmacies, how to identify the signs of rogue Internet pharmacies, as well as how to find safe Internet pharmacies. FDA officials told us that the agency plans to direct the same messages to health care professionals and assess the campaign's effectiveness in the future.

Some federal agencies and stakeholders have also taken steps to educate consumers about the risks of purchasing prescription drugs online and provide tools to help consumers identify legitimate and rogue Internet pharmacies. For example, CBP, DEA, and FTC post information on their websites regarding the dangers of purchasing drugs online.

---

[74]CBP has obtained this information through its Pharmaceuticals, Health & Chemicals Center of Excellence and Expertise—a program established in 2011 to better coordinate its activities with health industry stakeholders.

NABP publicly releases the results of its review of Internet pharmacies quarterly, which most recently showed that 97 percent of the over 10,000 Internet pharmacies that it reviewed were out of compliance with federal or state laws or industry standards.[75] NABP also warns consumers not to buy from websites that are on its publicly available list of rogue Internet pharmacies, and posts information on its website to educate consumers about how to safely buy medicine online.[76] The association directs consumers to purchase medicines from legitimate Internet pharmacies that it has accredited through its VIPPS program; as of May 1, 2013, NABP's website listed 32 VIPPS-accredited Internet pharmacies. To assist consumers in more readily identifying legitimate online pharmacies, NABP also plans to launch a new top-level domain name called *.pharmacy* by the end of 2013.[77] The association intends to grant this domain name to appropriately licensed, legitimate Internet pharmacies operating in compliance with regulatory standards—including pharmacy licensure, drug authenticity, and prescription requirements—in every jurisdiction that the pharmacy does business.

LegitScript also helps consumers to differentiate between legitimate and rogue Internet pharmacies. It regularly scans the Internet and, using NABP's standards, classifies Internet pharmacies into one of four categories: (1) legitimate, (2) not recommended, (3) rogue, or (4) pending review. When visiting their publicly available website, consumers can enter the website address of any Internet pharmacy and immediately find LegitScript's classification.[78] As of May 1, 2013, LegitScript had classified

---

[75]National Association of Boards of Pharmacy, *Internet Drug Outlet Identification Program, Progress Report for State and Federal Regulators: April 2013* (Mount Prospect, IL: Apr. 26, 2013).

[76]See http://www.nabp.net/programs/consumer-protection/buying-medicine-online/recommended-sites.

[77]A top-level domain name is the highest level of organizational structure on the Internet. Other top-level domain names include *.com*, *.net*, and *.gov*.

[78]See http://www.legitscript.com.

259 Internet pharmacies as legitimate and therefore safe for U.S. consumers, on the basis of NABP standards.[79]

Despite the actions of agencies and stakeholders, consumer education efforts face many challenges. Many rogue Internet pharmacies use sophisticated marketing methods to appear professional and legitimate, making it challenging for even well-informed consumers and health care professionals to differentiate between legal and illegal Internet pharmacies. For example, some rogue Internet pharmacies advertise that customers need a prescription in order to purchase drugs, but allow customers to meet this requirement by completing an online questionnaire at the time of sale. Other Internet pharmacies may fraudulently display a VIPPS-accreditation logo on their website, despite not having earned the accreditation, or may fraudulently display Visa, MasterCard, PayPal, or other logos on their website despite not holding active accounts with these companies or being able to process such payments. Figure 5 displays a screenshot of a rogue Internet pharmacy website that may appear to be legitimate to consumers, but whose operators pled guilty to multiple federal offenses, including smuggling counterfeit and misbranded drugs into the United States.

[79]The difference between NABP's count of 32 VIPPS-accredited Internet pharmacies and LegitScript's count of 259 legitimate Internet pharmacies, which are based on an application of the same criteria, may be attributed to the fact that pharmacies have to apply and send payment of fees to NABP for VIPPS accreditation, whereas they do not apply or send fees to LegitScript for classification. The VIPPS accreditation process requires an application fee and an annual participation fee that varies based on the type of pharmacy; application fees range from $5,000 to $8,000 and annual participation fees range from $1,000 to $7,000.

Figure 5: Screenshot of a Rogue Internet Pharmacy Website Whose Operators Pled Guilty to Multiple Federal Offenses, 2007

Source: Internet Archive.

Notes: The Food and Drug Administration, U.S. Immigration and Customs Enforcement, and the U.S. Postal Inspection Service conducted a joint investigation into this rogue Internet pharmacy, and in April 2012, its two operators pled guilty to smuggling counterfeit and misbranded drugs into the United States. We reviewed agency press releases, the indictments, and the court's judgments related to this investigation. The operators were prosecuted after federal agents conducted a series of undercover purchases from several of the operators' Internet pharmacies, including www.newpharm.net. Federal agents were able to purchase prescription medications without providing a valid prescription. Drugs were typically shipped to the United States from China and India, and exterior packaging typically falsely descr bed the contents of the shipments as "gifts" that had "no commercial value". The Internet pharmacy's website operators were located in Israel, customer service was located in the Philippines, and banking and money laundering were conducted in Cyprus and the Seychelles. Federal agents collaborated with law enforcement authorities in Hong Kong and Israel as part of the investigation. Laboratory results of drug samples purchased by federal agents revealed that the drugs were not genuine versions of the approved drugs that they purported to be. As part of their sentences, the operators were fined a total of $45,000 and forfeited a total of $65,000 as well as the domain names of their rogue Internet pharmacy websites. One of the operators was sentenced to 10 months of imprisonment, and the other was sentenced to 1 year of probation. *United States v. Carmi*, No. 11-CR-205 (E.D. Mo. 2012); *United States v. Dahan*, No. 11-CR-206 (E.D. Mo. 2012).

The image displayed is a screenshot of the www.newpharm.net website at as of June 25, 2007, as retrieved from http://web.archive.org/web/20070625062436/http://www.newpharm.net/ on June 5, 2013.

Some rogue Internet pharmacies seek to assure consumers of the safety of their drugs by purporting to be "Canadian." Canadian pharmacies have come to be perceived as a safe and economical alternative to pharmacies in the United States. Over the last 10 years, several local governments and consumer organizations have organized bus trips to Canada so that U.S. residents can purchase prescription drugs at Canadian brick-and-mortar pharmacies at prices lower than those in the United States. More recently, some state and local governments implemented programs that provided residents or employees and retirees with access to prescription drugs from Canadian Internet pharmacies.[80] Despite FDA warnings to consumers that the agency could not ensure the safety of drugs not approved for sale in the United States that are purchased from other countries, the prevalence of such programs may have contributed to a perception among U.S. consumers that they can readily save money and obtain safe prescription drugs by purchasing them from Canada. Many rogue Internet pharmacies seek to take advantage of this perception by purporting to be located in Canada, or sell drugs manufactured or approved for sale in Canada, when they are actually located elsewhere or selling drugs sourced from other countries.[81]

---

[80]For example, Maine recently enacted a law that allows licensed retail pharmacies located in Canada, the United Kingdom, Australia, and New Zealand to export prescription drugs to Maine residents for personal use without obtaining a license from the state. See 2013 Me. Legis. Serv. Ch. 373 (S.P. 60) (L.D. 171).

[81]A 2005 FDA study of drugs ordered from so-called "Canadian" Internet pharmacies found that 85 percent were from 27 other countries around the globe, and a number of these were counterfeit medicines.

Educational efforts also need to overcome issues related to consumer demand for these drugs. Many consumers mistakenly believe that if a drug may be prescribed for medical use, it is safe to consume regardless of whether they have a prescription for that particular drug.[82] In addition, other pressures, including consumers' desire to self-medicate, their wish for privacy related to obtaining lifestyle medications (such as drugs for sexual dysfunction), and relatively high out-of-pocket costs for brand-name drugs may fuel a demand among consumers to purchase prescription drugs from rogue Internet pharmacies. While educational efforts attempt to overcome these challenges, their success thus far is unknown—in part, because the volume of drugs purchased from rogue Internet pharmacies is unknown, making it difficult to assess whether educational efforts have been effective at reducing such purchases.

Agency Comments

We provided a draft of this report for comment to HHS, DOJ, and DHS, and we provided excerpts of this report for comment to USPIS and NSF. We received technical comments from HHS, DOJ, and DHS, which we incorporated as appropriate.

We are sending copies of this report to the Department of Commerce, the Department of Health and Human Services, the Department of Homeland Security, the Department of Justice, the Department of State, the Federal Trade Commission, the Internal Revenue Service, the National Science Foundation, the Office of Management and Budget, and the United States Postal Inspection Service, as well as other interested parties. In addition, the report is available at no charge on the GAO website at http://www.gao.gov.

---

[82]In addition to FDA's finding that nearly one in four Internet consumers residing in the United States have purchased prescription drugs online, the results of a recent survey suggest that 36 million—1 in every 6—Americans are estimated to have purchased at least one prescription drug online without a valid prescription. The Partnership at Drugfree.org, *Thirty-Six Million Americans Have Bought Medications Online Without a Doctor's Prescription* (Washington, D.C.: Dec. 14, 2010).

If you or your staff have any questions about this report, please contact me at (202) 512-7114 or crossem@gao.gov. Contact points for our Offices of Congressional Relations and Public Affairs may be found on the last page of this report. Other key contributors to this report are listed in appendix III.

Marcia Crosse
Director, Health Care

Appendix I: List of Organizations Interviewed

Federal Agencies	
	1. Department of Commerce, International Trade Administration
	2. Department of Commerce, National Telecommunications and Information Administration
	3. Department of Commerce, United States Patent and Trademark Office
	4. Department of Health and Human Services, Food and Drug Administration
	5. Department of Homeland Security, U.S. Customs and Border Protection
	6. Department of Homeland Security, U.S. Immigration and Customs Enforcement
	7. Department of Justice, Civil Division
	8. Department of Justice, Criminal Division
	9. Department of Justice, Drug Enforcement Administration
	10. Department of Justice, Executive Office for United States Attorneys
	11. Department of Justice, Federal Bureau of Investigation
	12. Department of State, Bureau of Economic and Business Affairs
	13. Department of State, Bureau of International Narcotics and Law Enforcement
	14. Federal Trade Commission
	15. Internal Revenue Service
	16. National Science Foundation
	17. Office of Management and Budget, Intellectual Property Enforcement Coordinator
	18. U.S. Postal Inspection Service
Selected State Boards of Pharmacy and Offices of Attorneys General	
	1. California
	2. Florida
	3. Maine
	4. Nevada
	5. Utah

Stakeholder Groups

1. AARP
2. Alliance for Safe Online Pharmacies
3. American Medical Association
4. American Well
5. Center for Safe Internet Pharmacies
6. Center for Telehealth and e-Health Law
7. Eli Lilly and Company
8. Federation of State Medical Boards
9. FedEx
10. Generic Pharmaceutical Association
11. Go Daddy
12. Google Inc.
13. International AntiCounterfeiting Coalition
14. Internet Crime Complaint Center
15. LegitScript
16. MasterCard International, Incorporated
17. Merck & Co., Inc.
18. Microsoft
19. National Alliance for Model State Drug Laws
20. National Association of Attorneys General
21. National Association of Boards of Pharmacy
22. National Association of Chain Drug Stores
23. National Community Pharmacists Association
24. National Cyber-Forensics & Training Alliance
25. National Science Foundation grant recipient Damon McCoy, Assistant Professor, George Mason University Computer Science Department
26. Partnership for Safe Medicines
27. PayPal
28. Pfizer
29. Pharmaceutical Security Institute

30. Pharmaceutical Research and Manufacturers of America

31. Purdue Pharma L.P.

32. Takeda Pharmaceuticals U.S.A., Inc.

33. UPS

34. Visa, Inc.

35. WellPoint, Inc.

Appendix II: Summary of Recent Proposals to Combat Rogue Internet Pharmacies

Members of Congress have sponsored bills and other stakeholders have endorsed proposals to enhance regulators' ability to both combat rogue Internet pharmacies and enhance the public's ability to distinguish rogue Internet pharmacies from legitimate ones. This appendix provides a brief synopsis of federal legislation introduced in the 112th Congress, which ran from January 2011 to January 2013, and the 113th Congress, from January 2013 through June 2013, as well as proposals from stakeholders we interviewed. While some stakeholders broadly supported these proposals, others noted that because most rogue Internet pharmacies are operated from overseas, additional federal laws and authorities, such as those noted below, would have a limited effect on their ability to combat rogue Internet pharmacies.

Creating a Federal Definition of a Valid Prescription. Some Members of Congress and other stakeholders have proposed creating a federal definition of a valid prescription that applies to all prescription drugs.[1] Currently, the only federal definition of a valid prescription applies solely to prescriptions for controlled substances.[2] Although the Federal Food, Drug, and Cosmetic Act (FDCA) requires certain drugs to be dispensed upon a prescription of a licensed practitioner, it does not define how this requirement is to be met. Instead, each state's pharmacy and medical practice acts define what constitutes a valid prescription. As such, when federal prosecutors pursue charges against operators of rogue Internet pharmacies that sell drugs without prescriptions that meet the FDCA's prescription requirement, they must research the laws of each relevant state to determine which ones apply to their case.

---

[1]For example, in the 112th Congress, Members of Congress introduced H.R. 4095 and S. 2002. Both bills were referred to as "The Online Pharmacy Safety Act." In addition to these bills, other stakeholders have recommended adopting a federal definition for a valid prescription, including the Intellectual Property Enforcement Coordinator as part of its work to coordinate federal efforts to combat pharmaceutical counterfeiting.

[2]The Ryan Haight Online Pharmacy Consumer Protection Act of 2008 instituted a federal definition of a valid prescription that applies to controlled substances, such as narcotic pain relievers. The act defines a valid prescription as one that is issued for a legitimate medical purpose in the usual course of professional practice, by a practitioner who has conducted at least one in-person medical evaluation of the patient, or a covering practitioner (who conducts a medical evaluation at the request of a temporarily unavailable practitioner who had conducted an in-person medical evaluation of the patient within the past 24 months). Certain telemedicine practices are permitted in place of an in-person medical evaluation. 21 U.S.C. § 829(e).

Proponents of a federal definition contend that such a definition would make it easier and less resource-intensive for federal and state investigators and prosecutors to gather evidence and build a case against rogue Internet pharmacy operators who sell drugs without valid prescriptions. Some contend, however, that such a definition would be of limited value. They note that, because rogue Internet pharmacy operations have increasingly moved components of their business abroad, they are beyond the boundaries of where such a law could be readily enforced. Additionally, those interested in promoting telemedicine have raised concerns that these proposals have too narrowly defined the circumstances for which prescriptions could be issued on the basis of legitimate medical examinations conducted via telemedicine.

Developing a Comprehensive List of Legitimate Internet Pharmacies. Members of Congress have introduced legislation that would have required the establishment of a comprehensive list of legitimate Internet pharmacies.[3] Other stakeholders, such as the Alliance for Safe Online Pharmacies, have also supported this proposal. Members of Congress and stakeholders have proposed that the Food and Drug Administration (FDA) would be responsible for establishing and maintaining the list.

Proponents of a comprehensive list contend that it would help consumers, stakeholders, and federal and state agencies distinguish between legitimate and rogue Internet pharmacies. Although the National Association of Boards of Pharmacy (NABP) and LegitScript have tools on their websites that enable consumers to identify legitimate Internet pharmacies, some maintain that FDA management of the list is critical, and could help to inspire public confidence in the list. Others stated that a list created by a third party would be helpful, as long as it is endorsed by the FDA. However, FDA officials and other stakeholders have raised concerns about the agency's ability to maintain such a list, given the large volume of new Internet pharmacies launched and modified every day. Additionally, FDA does not regulate the practice of pharmacy, which has long been regulated by the states. Finally, according to officials we interviewed from two stakeholders that provide services to Internet businesses, such a list is not necessary as their companies' policies and procedures allow them to immediately suspend customer accounts once

---

[3]The Online Pharmacy Safety Act (H.R. 4095 and S. 2002), introduced in the 112th Congress, included a provision for the establishment of a comprehensive list of legitimate Internet pharmacies.

they become aware that such customers are violating their policies and procedures.

Establishing a Safe Harbor for Companies That Provide Services to Internet-Based Businesses. Members of Congress have introduced legislation to provide legal immunity to companies—such as Internet registrars, search engines, and credit card processors—that ceased or refused to provide services to rogue Internet pharmacies when acting in good faith.[4] Proponents state that protection from liability would encourage companies to block services to rogue Internet pharmacies. In addition, some told us that such immunity would allow them to more readily take action against suspected rogue Internet pharmacies. However, others doubted the necessity of such legislation. Officials from two companies we interviewed explained that their companies already have the right to refuse service to rogue Internet pharmacies and do not open themselves up to liability by doing so.

Granting FDA New Subpoena and Seizure Authorities. Members of Congress have introduced legislation to grant new subpoena and seizure authorities to FDA. Agency officials stated the authorities would enable them to more rapidly investigate and take action against rogue Internet pharmacies.[5] Subpoena authority proposed under this legislation would have enabled FDA to compel the attendance and testimony of witnesses and the production of records and other items for the purposes of any hearing, investigation, or other proceeding related to a suspected FDCA violation. Further, seizure authority proposed under this legislation would have provided FDA with the authority to take noncompliant drugs out of the supply chain. At present, FDA must obtain approval from the Department of Justice (DOJ) in order to issue a subpoena or to seize goods. According to FDA officials, the DOJ approval process can delay investigations and enforcement actions. Such delays may lead to the

---

[4]In the 112th Congress, members of Congress introduced H.R. 3261, the Stop Online Piracy Act, and S. 968, the PROTECT IP Act of 2011, which contained similar safe-harbor provisions. The Online Pharmacy Safety Act (H.R. 4095 and S. 2002) also proposed a safe harbor and linked the provision to the establishment of a comprehensive list of legitimate Internet pharmacies. Companies would have been provided immunity for ceasing or refusing to provide services to Internet pharmacies not included on the list.

[5]The Drug Safety Enhancement Act of 2011, introduced in the 112th Congress as H.R. 1483, included provisions for subpoena authority (§ 404) and seizure authority (§ 205). The Drug Safety and Accountability Act of 2011, introduced in the 112th Congress as S. 1584, also included provisions for subpoena authority (§ 3).

distribution of noncompliant drugs further into the supply chain and may make such products more difficult to locate and seize.

Adopting a Track-and-Trace System for Prescription Drug Supply Chain. Members of Congress have introduced, and stakeholders such as the Intellectual Property Enforcement Coordinator have supported, legislation that would require FDA to implement a system to track, trace, and verify prescription drugs throughout the drug supply chain.[6] In 2007, Congress required FDA to develop standards that would apply to such a system, as well as to develop a standardized numerical identifier that could be applied to prescription drugs during manufacturing and repackaging.[7] In response, FDA issued guidance for industry, and hosted a public workshop on the topic. However, a nationwide track-and-trace system has not yet been implemented. Supporters of a nationwide track-and-trace system contend that it would enable federal agencies to more readily identify counterfeit or adulterated prescription drugs, as well as reduce the potential for counterfeit drugs to enter the supply chain, including through Internet pharmacies. FDA officials told us that while a track-and-trace system would benefit multiple stakeholders, it would likely not directly affect the operations of rogue Internet pharmacies because such enterprises sell counterfeit and adulterated drugs directly to consumers, which is not a distribution method that would be covered by a track-and-trace system.

---

[6]In the 113th Congress, members of Congress introduced H.R. 1919, the Safeguarding America's Pharmaceuticals Act of 2013, and S. 957, the Drug Supply Chain Security Act. Both bills would amend the FDCA to require that prescription drugs be tracked, traced, and verified throughout the supply chain. H.R. 1919 was passed by the House of Representatives on June 3, 2013, and was referred to the Senate Committee on Health, Education, Labor, and Pensions on June 4, 2013. The text of S. 957 was incorporated into S. 959 by the Senate Committee on Health, Education, Labor, and Pensions, and that bill was approved by the committee on May 22, 2013. The bill is pending consideration by the Senate as of June 17, 2013.

[7]See 21 U.S.C. § 355e (added by Pub. L. No. 110-85, § 913, 121 Stat. 823, 952 (2007)).

Appendix III: GAO Contact and Staff Acknowledgments

GAO Contact	Marcia Crosse, (202) 512-7114, crossem@gao.gov.
Staff Acknowledgments	In addition to the contact named above, Geri Redican-Bigott, Assistant Director; Michael Erhardt; Cathleen Hamann; Jason Kelly; Lisa Motley; Patricia Roy; and Lillian Shields made key contributions to this report.

Related GAO Products

Prescription Drug Control: DEA Has Enhanced Efforts to Combat Diversion, but Could Better Assess and Report Program Results. GAO-11-744. Washington, D.C.: August 26, 2011.

Intellectual Property: Observations on Efforts to Quantify the Economic Effects of Counterfeit and Pirated Goods. GAO-10-423. Washington, D.C.: April 12, 2010.

Cybercrime: Public and Private Entities Face Challenges in Addressing Cyber Threats. GAO-07-705. Washington, D.C.: June 22, 2007.

Intellectual Property: Better Data Analysis and Integration Could Help U.S. Customs and Border Protection Improve Border Enforcement Efforts. GAO-07-735. Washington, D.C.: April 26, 2007.

Internet Management: Prevalence of False Contact Information for Registered Domain Names. GAO-06-165. Washington, D.C.: November 4, 2005.

Anabolic Steroids Are Easily Purchased Without a Prescription and Present Significant Challenges to Law Enforcement Officials. GAO-06-243R. Washington, D.C.: November 3, 2005.

Prescription Drugs: Strategic Framework Would Promote Accountability and Enhance Efforts to Enforce the Prohibitions on Personal Importation. GAO-05-372. Washington, D.C.: September 8, 2005.

Internet Pharmacies: Some Pose Safety Risks for Consumers. GAO-04-820. Washington, D.C.: June 17, 2004.

Internet Pharmacies: Adding Disclosure Requirements Would Aid State and Federal Oversight. GAO-01-69. Washington, D.C.: October 19, 2000.

GAO's Mission	The Government Accountability Office, the audit, evaluation, and investigative arm of Congress, exists to support Congress in meeting its constitutional responsibilities and to help improve the performance and accountability of the federal government for the American people. GAO examines the use of public funds; evaluates federal programs and policies; and provides analyses, recommendations, and other assistance to help Congress make informed oversight, policy, and funding decisions. GAO's commitment to good government is reflected in its core values of accountability, integrity, and reliability.
Obtaining Copies of GAO Reports and Testimony	The fastest and easiest way to obtain copies of GAO documents at no cost is through GAO's website (http://www.gao.gov). Each weekday afternoon, GAO posts on its website newly released reports, testimony, and correspondence. To have GAO e-mail you a list of newly posted products, go to http://www.gao.gov and select "E-mail Updates."
Order by Phone	The price of each GAO publication reflects GAO's actual cost of production and distribution and depends on the number of pages in the publication and whether the publication is printed in color or black and white. Pricing and ordering information is posted on GAO's website, http://www.gao.gov/ordering.htm. Place orders by calling (202) 512-6000, toll free (866) 801-7077, or TDD (202) 512-2537. Orders may be paid for using American Express, Discover Card, MasterCard, Visa, check, or money order. Call for additional information.
Connect with GAO	Connect with GAO on Facebook, Flickr, Twitter, and YouTube. Subscribe to our RSS Feeds or E-mail Updates. Listen to our Podcasts. Visit GAO on the web at www.gao.gov.
To Report Fraud, Waste, and Abuse in Federal Programs	Contact: Website: http://www.gao.gov/fraudnet/fraudnet.htm E-mail: fraudnet@gao.gov Automated answering system: (800) 424-5454 or (202) 512-7470
Congressional Relations	Katherine Siggerud, Managing Director, siggerudk@gao.gov, (202) 512-4400, U.S. Government Accountability Office, 441 G Street NW, Room 7125, Washington, DC 20548
Public Affairs	Chuck Young, Managing Director, youngc1@gao.gov, (202) 512-4800 U.S. Government Accountability Office, 441 G Street NW, Room 7149 Washington, DC 20548

Please Print on Recycled Paper.

www.ingramcontent.com/pod-product-compliance
Lightning Source LLC
Chambersburg PA
CBHW080607290526
45790CB00007B/2668